# A MARVIN BELL READER

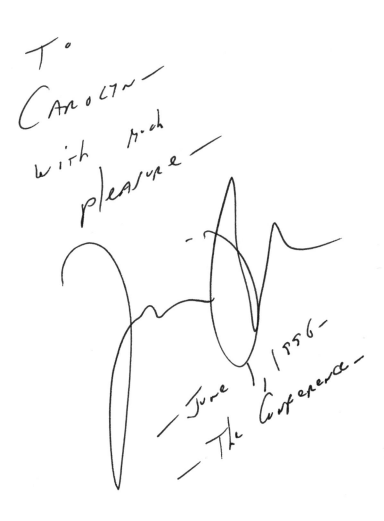

To
Carolyn—
with much
pleasure—

—June 1 1996—
—The Conference—

## The Bread Loaf Series of Contemporary Writers

MARVIN BELL

# A Marvin Bell
## READER

### SELECTED
### POETRY AND PROSE

*Middlebury College Press*
*Published by University Press of New England*
*Hanover and London*

MIDDLEBURY COLLEGE PRESS
Published by University Press of New England,
Hanover, NH 03755
© 1994 by Marvin Bell
All rights reserved
Printed in the United States of America   5   4   3   2   1

CIP data appear at the end of the book


COVER: Monotype by Marvin Bell.

This book is forever dedicated
to my wife, Dorothy Bell,
and to Nathan Bell and Jason Bell,
our sons.

One must imagine Sisyphus happy.

—ALBERT CAMUS

# Contents

POEMS

*Contents*

*Poems Within Essays*

''PAGES''

MEMOIRS

ESSAYS

A DEAD MAN SAMPLER

# A Bread Loaf Contemporary

A T  A  T I M E  when the literary world is increasingly dominated by commercial formulas and concentrated financial power, there is a clear need to restore the simple pleasures of reading: the experience of opening a book by an author you know and being delighted by a completely new dimension of her or his art, the joy of seeing an author break free of any formula to reveal the power of the well-written word. The best writing, many authors affirm, comes as a gift; the best reading comes when the author passes that gift to the reader, a gift the author could imagine only by taking risks in a variety of genres including short stories, poetry, and essays.

As editors of The Bread Loaf Series of Contemporary Writers we subscribe to no single viewpoint. Our singular goal is to publish writing that moves the reader: by the beauty and lucidity of its language, by its underlying argument, by its force of vision. These values are celebrated each summer at the Writers' Conference on Bread Loaf Mountain in Vermont and in each of these books.

We offer you the Bread Loaf Contemporary series and the treasures with which these authors have surprised us.

Robert Pack
Jay Parini

# Author's Preface

W H E N  Picasso was asked which of his paintings was his favorite, the story goes that he replied, "The next one." I can't imagine feeling any other way.

Writing is a form of talking to oneself. It is no exaggeration to say that I could not have survived as well without it. For ordinary talk, a walk will do. But talk that flings itself from a cliff to see if it can fly is another thing. I cherish the responses of others, but my poems begin as solitary, maverick investigations.

Now, in writing (as in conversation) I don't want to get fancy about epiphanies, enlightenment, the higher good and the greater good, belief, ecstasy, transformation, transcendence, evolution, or entropy. Rather, I want to get rabid about dirt and shoelaces, sex and sorrow. The one contains the other.

But the path toward the invisible can be twisty. In Heraclitean time, the moment passes. In a universe described by quantum physics, the presence of the observer affects what is observed. Flux and flow are where we find ourselves. Nor is the quality of mercy strained. As a writer, I begin, repeatedly, without knowing the end. Personally, I welcome this state of affairs. Whether we like it or not, knowing how little we know is the one constant, the source of our poetry, and the best hope for a better world.

What a thing to say!

This *Reader* brings back into print poems from seven out-of-print collections, including nine poems that did not appear in the *Selected*, and incorporates, also, a few poems from two books currently in print: *Iris of Creation* and *The Book of the Dead Man*. Thirteen other poems here are previously uncollected, as are the three sequences I call "Pages." Twelve poems appear within one of the memoirs and two of the essays.

Of the memoirs, two are reprinted from an out-of-print book of prose, while the third ("What Became What") is somewhat revised from a version that appeared in an autobiography series for which it was commissioned. Of the essays, "Noun/Object/Image" is from the aforementioned prose collection, while the other three are previously uncollected. Two of them, "The 'Technique' of Rereading" and "Three Propositions: Hooey, Dewey, and Loony," were first presented as lectures at the Bread Loaf Writers' Conference in 1982 and 1989, respectively. The anecdotal essay, "Bloody Brain Work," appeared originally as one in a series of columns in *The American Poetry Review*.

The writings gathered here were composed over thirty-two years, and consequently the reader will find overlaps. Conversely, some kinds of writings have been omitted in their entirety. I have chosen not to excerpt the book-length series *The Escape into You*, even though I did so for the *Selected*, since it now seems to me that it should remain discrete. Nor is there anything here from *Segues* or *Annie-over*, collections of poems co-written as correspondence. Finally, I have included no commissioned, occasional, or extra-long poems.

I could not resist making minor revisions.

I wish to thank Robert Pack, who suggested this *Reader*. I am glad to have had this reason to look back. Those poems and essays from even a few years ago appear to be the work of someone, or perhaps of several people, I used to know well. From now on, I will probably not be making the same sense that I used to.

M. B.

# POEMS

# The Self and the Mulberry

I wanted to see the self, so I looked at the mulberry.
It had no trouble accepting its limits,
yet defining and redefining a small area
so that any shape was possible, any movement.
It stayed put, but was part of all the air.
I wanted to learn to be there and not there
like the continually changing, slightly moving
mulberry, wild cherry and particularly the willow.
Like the willow, I tried to weep without tears.
Like the cherry tree, I tried to be sturdy and productive.
Like the mulberry, I tried to keep moving.
I couldn't cry right, couldn't stay or go.
I kept losing parts of myself like a soft maple.
I fell ill like the elm. That was the end
of looking in nature to find a natural self.
Let nature think itself not manly enough!
Let nature wonder at the mystery of laughter.
Let nature hypothesize man's indifference to it.
Let nature take a turn at saying what love is!

# White Clover

Once when the moon was out about three-quarters
and the fireflies who are the stars
of backyards
were out about three-quarters
and about three-fourths of all the lights
in the neighborhood
were on because people can be at home,
I took a not so innocent walk
out among the lawns,
navigating by the light of lights,
and there there were many hundreds of moons
on the lawns
where before there was only polite grass.
These were moons on long stems,
their long stems giving their greenness
to the center of each flower
and the light giving its whiteness to the tops
of the petals. I could say
it was light from stars
touched the tops of flowers and no doubt
something heavenly reaches what grows outdoors
and the heads of men who go hatless,
but I like to think we have a world
right here, and a life
that isn't death. So I don't say it's better
to be right here. I say this is where
many hundreds of core-green moons
gigantic to my eye
rose because men and women had sown green grass,
and flowered to my eye in man-made light,
and to some would be as fire in the body
and to others a light in the mind
over all their property.

# Unless It Was Courage

Again today, balloons aloft in the hazy *here*,
three heated, airy, basket-toting balloons,
three triangular boasts ahead against the haze
of summer and the gravity of onrushing fall—
these win me from the wavery *chrr*-ing of locusts
that fills these days the air between the trees,
from the three trembly outspreading cocoons hanging
on an oak so old it might have been weighed down
by the very thought of hundreds of new butterflies,
and from all other things that come in threes
or seem to be arranged. These *are* arranged,
they are the perfection of mathematics as idea,
they have lifted off by making the air greater—
nothing else was needed unless it was courage—
and today they do not even drag a shadow.

It was only a week ago I ran beneath one.
All month overhead had passed the jetliners,
the decorated company planes, the prop jobs
and great crows of greed and damage (I saw one
dangle a white snake from its bill as it flew),
and all month I had looked up from everywhere
to see what must seem from other galaxies
the flies of heaven. Then quickly my chance came,
and I ran foolish on the grass with my neck bent
to see straight up into the great resonant cavity
of one grandly wafting, rising, bulbous, whole
balloon, just to see nothing for myself. That
was enough, it seemed, as it ran skyward and away.
There I was, unable to say what I'd seen.
But I was happy, and my happiness made others happy.

# He Had a Good Year

while he was going blind. Autumnal light
gave to ordinary things the turning
beauty of leaves, rich with their losing.
A shade of yellow, that once stood opaque
in the rainbow of each glitzy morning,
now became translucent, as if the sun
broke against his own window. As for white,
it was now too much of everything,
as the flat deprivations of the color black
moved farther away: echoes of a surface
unseen and misremembered. I must tell you
how he managed as the lights went slowly out
to look inside the top glow of each object
and make in his mind a spectrum of inner
texture, of an essence isolate from the
nervous trembling of things struck by light.
"Ah, if God were only half the man he is,"
he said, "he would see things this way."

# Wednesday

Gray rainwater lay on the grass in the late afternoon.
The carp lay on the bottom, resting, while dusk took shape
in the form of the first stirrings of his hunger,
and the trees, shorter and heavier, breathed heavily upwards.
Into this sodden, nourishing afternoon I emerged,
partway toward a paycheck, halfway toward the weekend,
carrying the last mail and holding above still puddles
the books of noble ideas. Through the fervent branches,
carried by momentary breezes of local origin,
the palpable Sublime flickered as motes on broad leaves,
while the Higher Good and the Greater Good contended
as sap on the bark of the maples, and even I
was enabled to witness the truly Existential where it loitered
famously in the shadows as if waiting for the moon.
All this I saw in the late afternoon in the company of no one.

And of course I went back to work the next morning. Like you,
like anyone, like the rumored angels of high office,
like the demon foremen, the bedeviled janitors, like you,
I returned to my job—but now there was a match-head in my
    thoughts.
In its light, the morning increasingly flamed through the window
and, lit by nothing but mind-light, I saw that the horizon
was an idea of the eye, gilded from within, and the sun
the fiery consolation of our nighttimes, coming far.
Within this expectant air, which had waited the night indoors,
carried by—who knows?—the rhythmic jarring of brain tissue
by footsteps, by colors visible to closed eyes, by a music
in my head, knowledge gathered that could not last the day,
love and error were shaken as if by the eye of a storm,
and it would not be until quitting that such a man
might drop his arms, that he had held up all day since the dew.

# Who & Where

Where I live, it's a long uphill to
the Great Divide where larger men crossed
a streak in the land rivers know.
Somewhere else there may be gold in the trees
or dollars in the view. Here, we may be
nowhere ourselves but everywhere
on the way—so stop sometimes. We've eats,
nights, scars on the land, earth

you can pick up and squeeze,
the obvious. Sometimes we leave in
a line of dirt in a crack of skin.
If you drive past, you may see strange creatures
crossing the land, leaving behind them
heaps, bales, piles, clumps. And in the land:
supply lines, lost fingers, implements
left to rust where nothing now will grow.

2

Who I am is a short person with small feet
and fingers. When the hill is snowy,
I have to walk on the grass, and this gives
me a different viewpoint and wet shoes.
I see writers grow huge
in their writings. I get smaller yet,
so small that sometimes a tree is more
than I can look up to. I am down here with
all the other tiny, weak things. Sure,
once in a while I pull myself up
to assert something to the air, but oftener
I look for what was lost in the weeds.
The Gods drink nectar, I drink fruit juice.
All my life, people have told me,
"You are big, or will be." But I'm small.
I am not at the center of the circle.
I am not part of the ring. Like you,
I am not the core, the dark star or the lit star.
I take a step. The wind takes a step.
I take a drink of water. The earth swallows.
I just live here—like you, like you, like you.

# What Is There

When the grass, wet and matted,
is thick as a dry lawn is not,
I think of a kind of printing—
a page at a time, and the thick
paper hung up to dry, its
deep impressions filled and shapely
where ink is held and hardens.

And I wonder then at the underside
of those damp sheets of grass—
the muddy blood of those buried
coming up into the flattened green
as I press it underfoot, and pass,
and the sun drawing moisture
until we accept what is written there.

# Lightning

The roots of the tree are elastic, but
the huge elm wants to become
a cathedral—in a second more sudden,
more sudden than faith!—
which might have happened in just
such an instant: following the sign from the sky,
a homing flash and then
halves where there was one (tree, mind, way
of thinking, feeling). To contain a cathedral,

a tree must be very large, larger
than most. This one has the look of
a great event, a rupture (crusaders
could pray here), but *in*
*reality*, it has only the split personality
of the wooden saviour.

This is the present. Earlier,
I loved that old violin for winds, that tree,
that (like me) unpolished ladder
to this or that fine something I'll never see,
gone now to music.

# Trees as Standing for Something

### 1

More and more it seems I am happy with trees
and the light touch of exhausted morning.
I wake happy with her soft breath on my neck.
I wake happy but I am happier yet.
For my loves are like the leaves in summer.
But oh!, when they fall, and I wake with a start,
will I feel the sting of betrayal and ask, What is this
love, if it has to end, even in death,
or if one might lose it even during a life?
Who will care for such a thing?
Better to cut it down where it stands.
Better to burn it, and to burn with it,
than to turn around to see one's favorite gone.

### 2

It began when they cut down the elm and I let them.
When the corkscrew willow withered and I said nothing.
Then when the soft maple began to blow apart,
when the apple tree succumbed to poison,
the pine to a matrix of bugs, the oak to age,
it was my own limbs that were torn off, or so it seemed,
and my love, which had lived through many storms,
died, again and again. Again and again, it perished.
What was I to say then but Oh, Oh, Oh, Oh, Oh!
Now you see a man at peace, happy and happier yet,
with her breath on the back of his neck in the morning,
and of course you assume it must always have been this way.
But what was I to say, then and now, but Oh! and Oh! Oh!

# To No One in Particular

Whether you sing or scream,
the process is the same.
You start, inside yourself,
a small explosion, the difference
being that in the scream
the throat is squeezed so that
the back of the tongue
can taste the brain's fear.
Also, spittle and phlegm
are components of the instrument.
I guess it would be possible
to take someone by the throat
and give him a good beating.
All the while, though, some fool
would be writing down the notes
of the victim, underscoring
this phrase, lightening this one,
adding a grace note and a trill
and instructions in one of those languages
revered for its vowels.
But all the time, it's consonants
coming from the throat.
Here's the one you were throttling,
still gagging out the guttural ch—
the throat-clearing, Yiddish ch—
and other consonants spurned by
opera singers and English teachers.
He won't bother you again.
He'll scrape home to take it out
on his wife, more bestial consonants
rising in pitch until spent.
Then he'll lock a leg over her
and snore, and all the time
he hasn't said a word we can repeat.
Even though we all speak his language.
Even though the toast in our throats
in the morning has a word for us—

not at all like bread in rain,
but something grittier in something
thicker, going through what we are.
Even though we snort and sniffle,
cough, hiccup, cry and come
and laugh until our stomachs turn.
Who will write down this language?
Who will do the work necessary?
Who will gag on a chickenbone
for observation? Who will breathe perfectly
under water? Whose slow murder
will disprove for all time
an alphabet meant to make sense?
Listen! I speak to you in one tongue,
but every moment that ever mattered to me
occurred in another language.
Starting with my first word.
To no one in particular.

# He Said To

crawl *toward* the machine guns
except to freeze
for explosions and flares.
It was still ninety degrees
at night in North Carolina,
August, rain and all.
The tracer bullets wanted
our asses, which we swore to keep
down, and the highlight
of this preposterous exercise
was finding myself in mud
and water during flares. I
hurried in the darkness—
over things and under things—
to reach the next black pool
in time, and once
I lay in the cool salve that
so suited all I had become
for two light-ups of the sky.
I took one inside and one
face of two watches I ruined
doing things like that,
and made a watch that works.
From the combat
infiltration course and
common sense, I made a man
to survive the Army, which means
that I made a man to survive
being a man.

# The Uniform

Of the sleeves, I remember their weight, like wet wool,
on my arms, and the empty ends which hung past my hands.
Of the body of the shirt, I remember the large buttons
and larger buttonholes, which made a rack of wheels
down my chest and could not be quickly unbuttoned.
Of the collar, I remember its thickness without starch,
by which it lay against my clavicle without moving.
Of my trousers, the same—heavy, bulky, slow to give
for a leg, a crowded feeling, a molasses to walk in.
Of my boots, I remember the brittle soles, of a material
that had not been made love to by any natural substance,
and the laces: ropes to make prisoners of my feet.
Of the helmet, I remember the webbed, inner liner,
a brittle plastic underwear on which wobbled
the crushing steel pot then strapped at the chin.
Of the mortar, I remember the mortar plate,
heavy enough to kill by weight, which I carried by rope.
Of the machine gun, I remember the way it fit
behind my head and across my shoulder blades
as I carried it, or, to be precise, as it rode me.
Of tactics, I remember the likelihood of shooting
the wrong man, the weight of the rifle bolt, the difficulty
of loading while prone, the shock of noise.
For earplugs, some used cigarette filters or toilet paper.
I don't hear well now, for a man of my age,
and the doctor says my ears were damaged and asks
if I was in the Army, and of course I was but then
a wounded ear drum wasn't much in the scheme.

# Vietnam

is a place you will hear of
"in the future,"
which is not to say tomorrow merely,
over which a great peace
will have fallen, much as
the wool coverlet my love repaired
on my thirty-fifth Christmas
settles on my midday escapes to the couch.
This was a grimy coverlet, but pretty,
from the store of the Salvation Army
where I found too the long photo
of fading doughboys, the first tin soldiers,
and a loud five-buck castoff loveseat.
I hate to admit the uses we make of these:
nostalgia, sexual and so forth.
Another memento is a golden turtle-clock,
and when the alarm under its shell unwinds
some lot of time we marked is ended.
Though we know better about time,
we know nothing about peace,
which is a function of time and war
and which we can get from anything but people.

# We Tried to Stop the War

We tried to stop the war by standing up.
We emptied files and broke official seals.
We used skeleton keys on the closets in old houses.
Then we turned on a lamp to study the darkness.

We tried to stop the war by shutting our eyes.
The blast tore the retinas from oaken knotholes.
The blast ripped the ears from young guinea pigs.
So we turned on a lamp to study the darkness.

We tried to stop the war by going to war.
Our loyalty at night shocked even the owls.
We tried to stop the war by shining a light on it.
Then we turned on a lamp to study the darkness.

# Felt but Not Touched

That light behind the Olympics at supper hour—
it takes a sky of clouds from here to there
to spot the sun, seam and snow just right.
That pulsating light, a sizable incandescence
out of the grayness—that's the wing or tail of a plane.
The roundness of things—that's knowledge, a new way
to touch it here. (On the plains, we see Earth curve,
and I have seen the sun melt into the ocean elsewhere
and then call a color or two it left behind down.)

Then it is dark. The great streak of sunlight
that showed our side of snowy peaks has gone ahead.
Those bumps on the holly tree we passed
getting home for the late afternoon view from upstairs—
next to them, some smaller trees and a porch,
and next to that the streaky windows and then
the whole household getting ready to make the break
into spring—and sometimes in late winter we can't
sit still for connecting time at both ends.

If anything we do or don't will keep the world
for others, it will need such distant knowledge—beyond
experience, provable by ones, felt but not touched.
As we watch the light in the distance move on and around,
and the air at mountain height take up the cause of snow,
all that is beneath us that is not light has stopped.

Seattle

# Theory of Relativity (Political)

W H E N  I was young, dreaming of luminescent escapades set against the light of a great pearl hung in a sky that would otherwise be black, as if it were the one thing certain to survive the overwhelming forces of the tide of an invisible sea, I once thought of becoming a policeman but gave it up and became something else. Then one day the sea rose up and heaved itself from the sky, collapsing in exhaustion on the earth where it lay trying to catch its breath. From this I learned that the fiercest incandescence can be swallowed by accident if an open maw goes by, swimming or flying. From the cultivated moon today we must shift our attention to a speck of sand hung in an eye from which tears have fallen onto the earth and lie sighing. If we are going to be the world's policemen, we had better train for microcosms and the faces of wristwatches, for the damage one does in a small area just by turning around can cause tremors that travel by root and branch and spread like cracks in the crust of the desert. I and my countrymen, being patriotic, listen for organic pressures building under the surface, and in any event one does not want to play God when God plays God.

# What Songs the Soldiers Sang

Those with few images, lyrics
in which doing and undoing
prevailed, there were conclusions
and many epithets.
To hell with what it might look like!
The idea of breakfast, to take one
example, was a favorite
in the evenings. Also,
the way fields shut down,
and the weight of the equipment.
In choruses full of objects
nothing civilian moved
but loud young men bent on silence
and backbreaking labors.
It was natural to welcome them
with triumphal marches.
Many would return in halves.
The songs, too, about their singing, are lies.
The truth is that some songs were obscene
and that there were no words for others.

# March

I didn't play the trumpet today. Yesterday, I
thought about piano lessons again,
but lost the thought when the sun came out.
A clock looked over in a new way, I thought:
quizzically, its face kept me in view.
I had many things to do.

I wore some new shoes tight at the toe:
they changed my walk. And the dawn-leading light,
before the alarm could sound, enlivened
my step. I pushed the screen door against the house
extra hard in case the wind came back the wild way
it was yesterday.

As I walked into town, a refrain kept me company
somewhere inside, forming a cadence:
"Ask the Slavs, ask the Arabs,
ask the Africans, ask the Jews." In my near-waking,
I felt these were examples. I thought of dozens.
Some were cousins.

The refrain faded as I did my errands.
I could hardly hear it over the black ink of the newspaper.
The fruit I'd bought absorbed it, the meat I carried
muffled it, the bread encased it, and the paper bag rustled
against my shirt. Static over silence.
I felt the weight of my eyelids.

It was nothing, really. It was really nothing.
Branches and twigs lay all around because of yesterday's
storm. Storms have done worse
in deserts where no victim stood in place of trees.
Or, where victims stand, storms have had domain.
Wind and rain.

Is there any goodness left? I total it up:
the sun and moon, the food I bring from town,
many women and men, all children,
and the trees, of course. I don't know why they matter
unless it's their parental standing, and the words.
Or if it's that they make a place for birds.

# The Hole in the Sea

It's there
in the hole of the sea
where the solid truth lies,
written and bottled,
and guarded by limp-
winged angels—
one word under glass,
magnified by longing
and by the light tricks
of the moving man
in the moon.
Nights, that word shows,
up from the bottle,
up through the water,
up from the imaginable.
So that all who cannot
imagine, but yearn toward,
the word in the water,
finding it smaller
in the hole in the sea,
rest there. If no one
has drowned quite
in the hole of the sea,
that is a point
for theology. "Blame God
when the waters part,"
say sailors and Hebrews;
blame God, who writes us,
from His holy solution,
not to be sunk,
though all our vessels
convey black messages
of the end of the world.
So goes the story,
the storybook story, so goes
the saleable story:
Courage is in that bottle,
the driest thing there is.

# The Mystery of Emily Dickinson

Sometimes the weather goes on for days
but you were different. You were divine.
While the others wrote more and longer,
you wrote much more and much shorter.
I held your white dress once: 12 buttons.
In the cupola, the wasps struck glass
as hard to escape as you hit your sound
again and again asking Welcome. No one.

Except for you, it were a trifle:
This morning, not much after dawn,
in level country, not New England's,
through leftovers of summer rain I
went out rag-tag to the curb, only
a sleepy householder at his routine
bending to trash, when a young girl
in a white dress your size passed,

so softly!, carrying her shoes. It must be
she surprised me—her barefoot quick-step
and the earliness of the hour, your dress—
or surely I'd have spoken of it sooner.
I should have called to her, but a neighbor
wore that look you see against happiness.
I won't say anything would have happened
unless there was time, and eternity's plenty.

# The Poem

Would you like me more
if I were a woman?
Would you treat me better
were I a man?
I am just words, no
not words even, just marks
on a page, tokens of what?
Oh, you know.
Then tell them, will you.
Tell them to stop looking for me.
Tell them I never left home.
Tell them, if you must,
that I never left my body.
Unlike so many others,
I had no wings, just shoulders.
I was, like the snow bunting,
of stout build but moderate size.
Better make that "exceedingly" moderate size.
I neither blessed nor cursed
but that the good suffered
and evil closed the books in triumph.
I cured no one.
When I died, my bones
turned to dust, not diamonds.
At best, a tooth or two became coal.
How long it took.
You would have liked me then,
had you been alive still.
Had you survived
the silliness of the self,
you would have treated me better.
I never lied to you,
once I had grown up.
When x told you you were wonderful,
I said only that you existed.
When y said that you were awful,
I said only that life continues.

I did not mean a life like yours.
Not life so proud to be life.
Not life so conscious of life.
Not life reduced to this life or that life.
Not life as something—to see or own.
Not life as a form of life
which wants wings it doesn't have
and a skeleton of jewels,
not this one of bones and becoming.
How perfect are my words now,
in your absence!
Ungainly yet mild perhaps,
taking the place of no field,
offering neither to stand in the place of a tree
nor where the water was,
neither under your heel nor floating,
just gradually appearing,
gainless and insubstantial,
near you as always,
asking you to dance.

# An Introduction to My Anthology

Such a book must contain—
it always does!—a disclaimer.
I make no such. For here
I have collected all the best—
the lily from the field among them,
forget-me-nots and mint weed,
a rose for whoever expected it,
and a buttercup for the children
to make their noses yellow.

Here is clover for the lucky
to roll in, and milkweed to clatter,
a daisy for one judgment,
and a violet for when he loves you
or if he loves you not and why not.
Those who sniff and say no,
these are the wrong ones (and
there always are such people!)—
let them go elsewhere, and quickly!

For you and I, who have made it this far,
are made happy by occasions
requiring orchids, or queenly arrangements
and even a bird of paradise,
but happier still by the flowers of
circumstance, cattails of our youth,
field grass and bulrush. I have included
the devil's paint-brush
but only as a peacock among barn fowl.

# By Different Paths

We have all had our heads in a book
on the trouble with love
or, say, by a river looking for answers
downstream we have come to a place
somewhere inside us as smooth as
the guarded heart of an acorn
and how we came to be lost so
completely to one feeling
no one can say.

Ah, rules: of trees toward light
and water, cork and dead men to the surface,
some would say lunatics to the fringes.
But you and I, by different paths,
have arrived upstream from many possible
replies—I hope a craggy surface
won't prevent you—and the deaths we drop
stay down, lightheadedness also.
Now love is easy, pleases; no answer.

# Treetops

My father moves through the South hunting duck.
It is warm, he has appeared
like a ship, surfacing, where he floats, face up,
through the ducklands. Over the tops
of trees duck will come, and he strains
not to miss seeing the first of each flock,
although it will be impossible to shoot one
from such an angle, face up like that
in a floating coffin where the lid obstructs
half a whole view, if he has a gun.
Afterlives are full of such hardships.

One meets, for example, in one's sinlessness,
high water and our faithlessness,
so the dead wonder if they are imagined
but they are not quite.

How could they know we know
when the earth shifts deceptively
to set forth ancestors to such pursuits?
My father will be asking, Is this fitting?
And I think so—I, who, with the others,
coming on the afterlife after the fact
in a dream, in a probable volume, in a
probable volume of dreams, think so.

# Trees Standing Bare

Those that do are not ashamed
to stand without leaves through the winter.
They know that loneliness
is not a clover pasture
or a stand of oak and hickory. They know
that the green of a pine
is all we will know of green,
and that all we will know of the dark
is sleep's forgetfulness.

# Written During Depression:
# How to Be Happy

To be happy,
a man must love death
and failure. Then,
however great the flash
of this moment or that bit
of life's work, there
will come always another moment
to be appreciated because
fading or crumbling. If,
however, a man loves
life, there can be no end to it,
nor hope. If a man loves
reason, eventually he
will find none. If he loves
the interest of others,
he will be made to apologize
continually for his own being.
If he loves form, all
that he does or knows will
come, not to nothing, but
to that other possibility
of meaninglessness: everything.
That is why "the shape of things
to come" is a phrase littered with
tracks into the bush
where the pure primitive
is a headhunter's delusion,
and why, my dear, I love you.

# Stars Which See, Stars Which Do Not See

They sat by the water. The fine women
had large breasts, tightly checked.
At each point, at every moment,
they seemed happy by the water.
The women wore hats like umbrellas
or carried umbrellas shaped like hats.
The men wore no hats and the water,
which wore no hats, had that well-known
mirror finish which tempts sailors.
Although the men and women seemed at rest
they were looking toward the river
and some way out into it but not beyond.
The scene was one of hearts and flowers
though this may be unfair. Nevertheless,
it was probable that the Seine had hurt them,
that they were "taken back" by its beauty
to where a slight breeze broke the mirror
and then its promise, but never the water.

# To Dorothy

You are not beautiful, exactly.
You are beautiful, inexactly.
You let a weed grow by the mulberry
and a mulberry grow by the house.
So close, in the personal quiet
of a windy night, it brushes the wall
and sweeps away the day till we sleep.

A child said it, and it seemed true:
"Things that are lost are all equal."
But it isn't true. If I lost you,
the air wouldn't move, nor the tree grow.
Someone would pull the weed, my flower.
The quiet wouldn't be yours. If I lost you,
I'd have to ask the grass to let me sleep.

# Trinket

I love watching the water
ooze through the crack in the fern pot,
it's a small thing

that slows time
and steadies
and gives me ideas of becoming

having nothing to do
with ambition or even reaching,
it isn't necessary at such times

to describe this,
it's no image for mean keeping,
it's no thing that small

but presence.
Other men look at the ocean,
and I do too,

though it is too many
presences for any
to absorb.

It's this other,
a little water, used, appearing
slowly around the sounds

of oxygen and small frictions,
that gives the self
the notion of the self

one is always losing
until these tiny embodiments
small enough to contain it.

# These Green-Going-to-Yellow

This year,
I'm raising the emotional ante,
putting my face
in the leaves to be stepped on,
seeing myself among them, that is;
that is, likening
leaf-vein to artery, leaf to flesh,
the passage of a leaf in autumn
to the passage of autumn,
branch-tip and winter spaces
to possibilities, and possibility
to God. Even on East 61st Street
in the blowzy city of New York,
someone has planted a gingko
because it has leaves like fans like hands,
hand-leaves, and sex. Those lovely
Chinese hands on the sidewalks
so far from delicacy
or even, perhaps, another gender of gingko—
do we see them?
No one ever treated us so gently
as these green-going-to-yellow hands
fanned out where we walk.
No one ever fell down so quietly
and lay where we would look
when we were tired or embarrassed,
or so bowed down by humanity
that we had to watch out lest our shoes stumble,
and looked down not to look up
until something looked like parts of people
where we were walking. We have no
experience to make us see the gingko
or any other tree,
and, in our admiration for whatever grows tall
and outlives us,
we look away, or look at the middles of things,
which would not be our way
if we truly thought we were gods.

# Gemwood

*to Nathan and Jason*

In the *shoppes*
they're showing "gemwood":
the buffed-up flakes of dye-fed pines—
bright concentrics or bull's-eyes,
wide-eyed on the rack of
this newest "joint effort
of man and nature." But then

those life-lines circling
each target chip of "gemwood"
look less like eyes, yours or mine,
when we have watched a while.
They are more like the whorls
at the tips of our fingers,
which no one can copy. Even on

the photocopy Jason made of
his upraised hands, palms down
to the machine, they do not appear.
His hands at five-years-old—
why did we want to copy them, and
why does the gray yet clear print
make me sad? That summer,

the Mad River followed us
through Vermont—a lusher state than
our own. A thunderous matinee
of late snows, and then the peak
at Camel's Hump was bleached.
As a yellow pear is to the sky—
that was our feeling. We had with us

a rat from the lab—no, a pet
we'd named, a pure friend who changed
our minds. When it rained near
the whole of the summer, in that
cabin Nathan made her a social creature.
She was all our diversion, and brave.
That's why, when she died

in the heat of our car
one accidental day we didn't intend,
it hurt her master first and most,
being his first loss like that,
and the rest of our family felt badly
even to tears, for a heart that small.
We buried her by the road

in the Adirondack Mountains,
and kept our way to Iowa.
Now it seems to me the heart
must enlarge to hold the losses
we have ahead of us. I hold to
a certain sadness the way others
search for joy, though I like joy.

Home, sunlight cleared the air
and all the green's of consequence. Still
when it ends, we won't remember
that it ended. If parents must receive
the sobbing, that is nothing
when put next to the last crucial fact
of who is doing the crying.

# Starfish

H I S  entire body is but one hand, severed at the wrist. It lies on the sand in the late afternoon as if sunning itself. As he dries, he reaches ever more arthritically for the light itself with which to brown his palm. In this regard, his futility is unsurpassed.

You may pick him up now. Dead hand in your live hand. The mount of flesh just behind the thumb has been planed down and the soft tissue, tissue that will never tan, seems to have endured much scraping and dragging on the roughest edges of the sea, and to have fought back by raising its hackles, as it were, until it has become a hand of tiny spikes, but spikes nonetheless. Rub him in your palm, if you like. His hand is tougher than your own.

Of course, this starfish that we know is only the version run aground, becalmed, out of its element, preserved, petrified. In its lifetime, which we have missed entirely, it was soft, it was spongy, it was bread to the sea. Then, it molded itself to its element, water, not as a hand closes around a prized possession to become a fist, but as a wheel becomes motion without losing its shape even for a moment.

The starfish, alive, was a kind of wheel. The sea was its air, as all around us in what we call a universe are stars in space like fish in the ocean. Like fish, we know them only at a distance, we approach closer to them by means of glass and mirrors, we grow silent in the presence of the mysterious nature of them, we may only imagine touching them when they have been cast up on the beach or thrown down from light.

Such is our conception of Heaven, from which it seems we are forever finding souvenirs, signals, clues. We have no way of knowing whether, at any single moment, we are being led toward a Heaven that follows upon our lives or toward one that precedes it, or indeed whether or not these may be the same. Is it not then natural that we look down in the light and up in the darkness, and is it not also ironic that it requires a dark, absorbent object to stop our gaze in the former while it takes a moment of hard light to focus us in the latter? We shall never know the end of our thoughts, nor where they began.

Return to our starfish now. Time has given it a new, earthy odor.

# After a Line by Theodore Roethke

*In the vaporous grey of early morning,*
on the mudflats of the moon, in grey feeling,
walking among boulders uncovered by minus-tides,
I am also still in the still hallway of dream,
facing a stairway without end, in a night without wires,
some recollection hanging in the air, whose image,
unapproachable in the night, waits out there.

Nothing to be gained but rain, and the burning of rain,
this day beginning with such thirst, such capacity
that everything may come to be again in reverse:
a world uncreated, a planet no one is watching—
not even we ourselves—now rising out of misty nothingness,
so that first stones are not solitary nor beings lonely,
nor water divided, nor continents discrete.

Joy to be wordless yet wide awake,
walking by water, in the midst of an unsubstantial suspense,
in clear sight of mist, in mud that sponges up the way back,
in the sight of the closed eyes of one still sleeping,
and there to be gathering shape and form
like a long whip of seaweed being inexorably washed ashore,
and now a head of hair stirring to bring love back which was gone.

# The Stones

One night in my room
many stones brought together over the years,
each bearing the gouges and pinpricks
of sea and shore life,
and each weighted according to the sea
which first chisels a slate
and then washes it and later writes on it
with an eraser—
these stones, large and small, flat,
rounded, conical, shapely or rough-hewn,
discussed their origins,
and then got around to me. One of them,
the white one full of holes
that wipes off on your hands, said
that he thinks I carry much sadness,
the weight of a heart full of stones,
and that I bring back these others
so that I might live among the obvious
heaviness of the world.
But another said that I carried him
six months in Spain
in a pants pocket and lifted him out
each night to place on the dresser,
and although he is small and flat,
like a planet seen from the moon,
I often held him up to the light,
and this is because I am able to lift
the earth itself. And isn't this
happiness? But a third stone spoke
from where it stood atop papers
and accused me of trying to manage
the entire world, which for the most part
is neither myself nor not myself,
and is also the air around the rim
of a moving wheel, the space beyond Space,
the water within water,
and the weight within the stone.

Then they all asked what right had I
to be happy or unhappy,
when the language of stones
was no different
from the language of a white lump of dung
among the excellent vegetables.

# Victim of Himself

He thought he saw a long way off the ocean
cresting and falling, bridging the continents,
carrying the whole sound of human laughter
and moans—especially moans, in the mud of misery—
but what he saw was already diluted, evaporating,
and what he felt were his teeth grinding
and the bubbles of saliva that broke on his tongue.

He was doomed to be a victim of himself.
He thought he saw, in the future, numberless, cavernous
burials—the outcome of plagues, of wars,
of natural disasters created by human beings—
but what he saw was already faded, disintegrating,
and what he felt was the normal weakness displayed
by droopy eyes and muscles that bleated meekly.

He thought he saw from Earth up to the stars
and from any one moment back to the hour of his birth
when desire produced, in the slush of passionate tides,
a citizen of mud and ash, of lost light and dry beds,
but what he saw was already distorted, moving away,
and what he felt was a sense of loss that so often
he had been at peace in her arms when he did not
    intend to be.

# Temper

The seed, in its grave,
is the firmest line of labor.
A man woos havoc to undertake
the destruction of a dam in a drought.

Weren't you wound up to be metal
rulers for the hocus-pocus?
The great face of the earth
is pained to be nothing without you:

a sopping interdependence
to make bricks from mud and a family
from seed, and anger
clear through to the center.

# My Hate

My hate is like ripe fruit
from an orchard, which is mine.

I sink my teeth into it.
I nurse on its odd shapes.

I have grafted every new variety,
walked in my bare feet,

rotting and detached,
on the fallen ones.

Vicious circle. Unfriendly act.
I am eating the whole world.

In the caves of my ill will
I must be stopped.

# The Condition

The darkness within me is growing.
I am turned out.

Thought feeds on it
even as the body is eaten.

Its goodness is without a face.
But it convinces me to look.

It can fade from now until doomsday.
It will not fade.

In the night I see it shining,
like a thing seen.

# The Parents of Psychotic Children

They renounce the very idea
of information, they are enamored
of the notion of the white tablet.
Their babies were outrageously beautiful
objects exploding their lives,
moving without compensation
because of them to worlds without them.
They believe they were presented
inadequate safeguards, faulty retribution,
and a concerted retirement into crime
of the many intent on their injury.
No two can agree on the miraculous
by which they were afflicted,
but with economy overcome
their fears of the worst. Their children, alas,
request nothing. And the far-fetched doctors,
out of touch with the serious truth,
are just practical and do not sing,
like the crazy birds, to their offspring.

# Things We Dreamt We Died For

Flags of all sorts.
The literary life.
Each time we dreamt we'd done
the gentlemanly thing,
covering our causes
in closets full of bones
to remove ourselves forever
from dearest possibilities,
the old weapons re-injured us,
the old armies conscripted us,
and we gave in to getting even,
a little less like us
if a lot less like others.
Many, thus, gained fame
in the way of great plunderers,
retiring to the university
to cultivate grand plunder-gardens
in the service of literature,
the young and no more wars.
Their continuing tributes
make them our greatest saviours,
whose many fortunes are followed
by the many who have not one.

# The Politics of an Object

T H E  banana is stronger than the human head in the following ways: those fine threads that wave from the top knot are harder to break than hair. Should you pick one up, you cannot resist peeling it: it will have done to it what it was born to have done to it. As for endurance and sacrifice: while thousands of well-muscled laborers did not survive the cheap labor of imperialism in their republics, and others died with their mouths stuffed full of money, the banana hung on, gathering potassium. It knew the future, it knew its history, it was prepared for bruises. I have gathered the small colorful stickers applied one to a bunch until now they cover the wooden arms of the chair where I often linger in the kitchen to chat with my wife. The bananas don't last long, eaten or not. But each of the tiny stickers, each company logo, stays in place incorruptibly, and, though I am but one man, without a plan, I am keeping their names in mind. So you see? A banana is superior to a human head because it gives up without a fight. And still there is a future.

# The Hen

hungers to whistle. She longs to hear a cry ring out
from all the bottled-up mothers. At dawn
in the barnyard, see her throat squeeze
from the effort, and her clumpy body go up on tiptoe
to reach a higher register. Hear the gravel rattle
in her craw as she croaks her egg song.
She is the ballerina of ballerinas, the queen
of torch, the damsel in distress sure to be saved
for her great beauty, her way with music
and the frilly glow of freedom in her feathers.

The rooster, on flat feet. He feels like a policeman
inside a whistle, seeing the robbers
make off with the loot. While she feels like a wife in port
watching for a ship in a bottle. O anger suffused
by clucking and scratching, oh hunger that rings, dashing
itself on the stones of a common indigestion—
or else she will be asked to walk a line in the dirt
so that she might be hypnotized for the ax!
The hen knows hunger is a bag of bones. She has
a straw mattress and an underestimated egg.

# Jane Was with Me

Jane was with me
the day the rain dropped a squirrel *like that*.
An upside-down embrace,
a conical explosion from the sky,
a thick flowering of sudden water—
whatever it was,
the way it happened is
that first the trees grew a little,
and then they played music
and breathed songs and applauded themselves,
and that made the squirrel
surrender to nothing but the beauty
of a wet tree
about to shake its upper body like the devil.
And of course, of course,
he went out on that tree just as far as he could
when things were not so beautiful
and that was it: hard onto the roof of our car
before he could set his toes.

The flat whack of the body.
He lay in the street breathing and bleeding
until I could get back,
and then he looked me in the eye exactly.
Pasted to the concrete by his guts,
he couldn't lift, or leave, or live.
And so I brought the car and put its right tire
across his head. If in between
the life part and the death part,
there is another part,
a time of near-death,
we have come to know its length and its look
exactly—in this life always near death.
But there's something else.
Jane was with me.
After the rain, the trees were prettier yet.

And if I were a small animal with a wide tail,
I would trust them too. Especially
if Jane were with me.

# Dew at the Edge of a Leaf

The broader leaves collect
enough to see early
by a wide spread of moonlight,
and they shine!, shine!—
who are used to turning
faces to the light.

Looking up is farthest.
From here or under any tree,
I know what will transpire:
leaves in their watery halos have
an overhead-to-underfoot career,
and thrive toward falling.

In a passage of time and water,
I am half-way—a leaf in July?
In August? I take no pity.
Everything green is turning brown,
it's true, but then too
everything turning brown is green.

# The Nest

The day the birds were lifted from my shoulders,
the whole sky was blue, a long-imagined effect
had taken hold, and a small passenger plane
was beating the earth with its wings
as it swung over the bean fields toward home.
A fat car barely traveled a narrow road
while I waited at the bottom of a hill.
People around me were speaking loudly
but I heard only whispers, and stepped away.

You understand, I was given no choice.
For a long time, I was tired of whatever it was
that dug its way into my shoulders for balance
and whispered in my ears, and hung on for dear life
among tall narrow spaces in the woods
and in thickets and crowds, like those of success,
with whom one mingles at parties and in lecture halls.
In the beginning, there was this or that . . .
but always on my shoulders that which had landed.

That was life, and it went on in galleries
and shopping plazas, in museums and civic centers,
much like the life of any responsible man
schooled in the marriage of history and culture
and left to learn the rest at the legs of women.
In furtive rooms, in passing moments, the sea
reopened a door at its depth, trees spoke
from the wooden sides of houses, bodies became
again the nests in the naked tree.

After that, I was another person,
without knowing why or how, and after that,
I lived naked in a new world where the sun
broke through windows to grasp entire families
and crept between trees to wash down streets
without disturbing any object, in a world
where a solitary kiss blew down a door.
The day the birds were lifted from my shoulders,
it killed me—and almost cost me a life. . . .

# A Man May Change

As simply as a self-effacing bar of soap
escaping by indiscernible degrees in the wash water
is how a man may change
and still hour by hour continue in his job.
There in the mirror he appears to be on fire
but here at the office he is dust.
So long as there remains a little moisture in the stains,
he stands easily on the pavement
and moves fluidly through the corridors. If only one
cloud can be seen, it is enough to know of others,
and life stands on the brink. It rains
or it doesn't, or it rains and it rains again.
But let it go on raining for forty days and nights
or let the sun bake the ground for as long,
and it isn't life, just life, anymore, it's living.
In the meantime, in the regular weather of ordinary days,
it sometimes happens that a man has changed
so slowly that he slips away
before anyone notices
and lives and dies before anyone can find out.

# Days of Time

*Gone into the woods*, they'll say, only because
I preferred the company of trees, any kind of tree,
to the company of . . . . It was a day like this one,
in the dark season, a time when one sits in the center
avoiding the flat wind that blows through the walls,
that time when icy vapors hover above the river
and the big pines move like old men in dark clothes
for an important occasion: the days of time, time of time.

*Gone into the sea*, they'll say, just because
I loved to walk on the darkened sand at the weed line
near to the scalloped edge of the ocean, and there
felt on the soles of my feet as the spent waves receded
the termites of ocean floors and the crab imprint
that gives the galaxy a picture of the galaxy.
It was a wide day in the sunshine, but narrow in the shadows,
when I walked around a bend in the beach and stayed.

*Disappeared into thin air*, they'll say, because
I stopped to look up at a giant red fan in the clouds
and a picture of four bakers peeking over the horizon,
and counted the wooden thread-spools in a cigar box.
It was a day like this one: sulphur hung in the air,
somewhere the earth vented the steam at its core.
It was a day in the future, just like this in the future,
when the melting wax no longer seemed to betray the candle.

# Two Pictures of a Leaf

If I make up this leaf
in the shape of a fan, the day's cooler
and drier than any tree. But if
under a tree I place before me
. this same leaf as on a plate,
dorsal side up and then its ribs
set down like the ribs of a fish—
then I know that fish are dead to us
from the trees, and the leaf
sprawls in the net of fall to be
boned and eaten while the wind gasps.
Ah then, the grounds are a formal ruin
whereon the lucky who lived
come to resemble so much that does not.

# Sevens (Version 3): In the Closed Iris of Creation

A pair of heavy scissors lay across the sky
waiting for an affirmation,
waiting for the go-ahead of tragic love.
The sky, as always, was full of sobbing clouds
ready to rain down heavily on desire
wherever a hand opens or a leg stretches out
and life waits to begin—
the way everything, even scissors, waits to begin.
We who began in water, in clay,
in the ancient diggings of the word,
whitened by the chalk of dreams,
bloom in colors (everyone has noticed!)
blind toward scissors and clouds.
Within the sight of a pail of water,
our mothers pushed us away
for the good of our souls
into a world where the sun had burned a hole
in the name of love.
Now sleep in the sewers
descends, bringing us an inner life
at peace behind an in-turning iris—
crawling, pre-cadaverous, fetal.
To choose between knowing the truth
or, on the other hand, orgasm and repose,
always like a cricket on guard
in case Spring should arrive in disguise,
hiding its muscular body under rags,
its footsteps muffled by the mating of vines—
to choose at all, we have to crawl
on bare knees down alleys of pumice
and plead among the red columns of silos,
in the dust of exploding grains,
with shaking hands and trembling lips
plead for a severing of the knives.
If now in the black hole we sometimes dance

like orphans among new loaves of bread,
and lift plain water to toast
our good luck, and if in a thicket of almonds
bearing the smell of oil before it turns
to bitter wine,
we laugh so hard we lose our bodies momentarily,
we are also, at the same time, absorbing
the shivering of the cities
born of this baked earth, this chaste diamond
that flowered, reluctantly, absurdly,
into an eternity of ice
and descended through the decorations of the frost
to be shipwrecked in space.
Thus, each morning I throw a little chalk into my coffee
in memory of the blood and bones of the universe,
and each day I eat some sacramental bread
as a prayer
not to become one of the thieves
but to save and keep my life for whenever I may need it,
perhaps when things are going better,
when everything is or isn't sevens,
and the planet is in perpetual motion
giving continuous birth to the space behind her.
I myself swear never to be surprised
when someone tries to stay in the womb.
The great silence that filled the Void
was grounded by the first rain,
beaten into piles of grain and no grain
in the first silo, in the first air,
without a place to put a foot down, without an us,
all in a hole
that held (aloft? upside down?) as if in an iris
the thin tracings of the first wax,
and of the first delicate amoebic embracings,
and of the shapes to come when love
began to sever us.

# Little Father Poem

We must stay away from our fathers,
who have big ears. We must stay away
from our fathers, who are the snow.
We must avoid the touch of the leaves
who are our proud fathers. We must
watch out for father underfoot. Father
forgave us when we did nothing wrong,
Father made us well when we were healthy,
now Father wants to support us
when we weigh nothing, Father in his grave
gives us everything we ever wanted,
in a boat crossing who-knows-where,
mist flat over the water,
the sand smooth because soft.

# Water, Winter, Fire

In the little light of dawn
the mercantile ships of Rome
slide into the breakers.
A rain of waves will hide them
forever beneath our dream.
We have always known of
the buried life, of these sources
of treasure, and of the washing—
the washing we have known.

———————

Suddenly, where leaves were,
there is nothing. The seasons
have shifted above us
in an indistinct rustle—
frozen, finally, to silence.
We had always suspected
the dying of all fruit,
and the likelihood of turning
poisonous during the night.

———————

Now that building, which has burned
so often, is burning again.
Our books and papers are rising
irretrievably into the heavens.
Heavier things are up and falling,
for which there can be no helping.
We have dreamt in this life before:
now, suddenly, the air is burning;
now it is useless to be home.

# Introduction

Just as this is no time to be bringing up the subject,
today the benefits of the family concern us,
though surely the subject shall suffer in the midst of discussion
in its absence. As what proceeds proceeds by opposites,
the subconscious upward-floating as always if left alone
with its squiggly comics-characters
not looking at all like the hot toads of the surrealists,
so it is clear that a study, say, of the eagle
will describe America completely by taking the eye
of the student into the sky anywhere, zingy!
And research into the family, which is just ending,
starts here. For here we are equals in poverty,
unless you have brought along more than appears.
Take your hands from your pockets and wear them openly.
All that's required's good posture, by which
we mean a mind that does not slump nor bow beneath feet.
Our intention, unfashionable, is to be wise.
One hopes the terrain will not prove familiar,
though the safety devices we have packed and packed may
ruin our sincere hopes of finding a new place.
Still, we set out with our hearts, which are good,
and our teachers' warnings uncorrected by experience.
Wish us well. For now we are in danger, from ourselves.

# On the Word "Posture" in the Preceding

Art is to life, today, as beauty/history is to fact.
We may invoke the authority of either.
Sufficiency of argument is lovely ours in either case!
The word "posture" in the foregoing
derives from history as biography does not. In "plain"
truth, no one ever lived as supposed.
The biography, a posture, approximates a man
with ticklish ribs, a shrew for a witch doctor
and a deep-seated need to bully the sublime, whooey.
Phew! Tired of the place and people, where's to go?
Thus, it is preferable to be far-and-away "not tired of."
No fatigue, in fact, will afflict us if we adopt
posture, and give up on our biographies. Still,
we may often be tired in art, faint wisdom,
in works made from weakness, neurosis and crisis—
as if an island could be made from the just-departed sands!
Oh no. Here comes the dredger where I lived,
to clear the channel the length of my childhood.

# The Last Thing I Say

to a thirteen-year-old sleeping,
tone of an angel, breath of a soft wing,
I say through an upright dark space
as I narrow it pulling the door
sleepily to let the words go surely into
the bedroom until I close them in
for good, a nightwatchman's-worth
of grace and a promise for morning
not so far from some God's first notion
that the world be an image by first light
so much better than pictures of hope
drawn by firelight in ashes,
so much clearer, too, a young person
wanting to be a man might draw one finger
along an edge of this world and it
would slice a mouth there
to speak blood and then should he put that wound
into the mouth of his face,
he will be kissed there and taste
the salt of his father as he lowers
himself from his son's high bedroom
in the heaven of his image of
a small part of himself and sweet dreams.

# Instructions to Be Left Behind

I've included this letter in the group
to be put into the cigar box—the one
with the rubber band around it you will find
sometime later. I thought you might
like to have an example of the way in which
some writing works. I may not say anything
very important or phrase things just-so,
but I think you will pay attention anyway
because it matters to you—I'm sure it does,
no one was ever more loved than I was.

What I'm saying is, your deep attention
made things matter—made art,
made science and business
raised to the power of goodness, and sport
likewise raised a level beyond.
I am not attaching to this a photograph
though no doubt you have in your mind's eye
a clear image of me in several expressions
and at several ages all at once—which is
the great work of imagery beyond the merely
illustrative. Should I stop here for a moment?

These markings, transliterations though they are
from prints of fingers, and they from heart
and throat and corridors the mind guards,
are making up again in you the one me
that otherwise would not survive that manyness
daisies proclaim and the rain sings much of.
Because I love you, I can almost imagine
the eye for detail with which you remember
my face in places indoors and out and far-flung,
and you have only to look upwards to see
in the plainest cloud the clearest lines
and in the flattest field your green instructions.

Shall I rest a moment in green instructions?
Writing is all and everything, when you care.
The kind of writing that grabs your lapels
and shakes you—that's for when you don't care
or even pay attention. This isn't that kind.
While you are paying your close kind of attention,
I might be writing the sort of thing you think
will last—as it is happening, now, for you.
While I was here to want this, I wanted it,
and now that I am your wanting me to be myself
again, I think myself right up into being
all that you (and I too) wanted me to be: You.

# The Pill

T H E  pill, in the pill bottle, humming like a wheel at rest, confident that the time must come when it will control the future and distance unravel to the end of time—this small round package of power, this force for lingering life or lingering death, this salt for the soul, this spice with roots in antiquity—this coated equation smaller than a fingertip embodies and contains you. And who gave it that right, who harnessed chemistry and put *things* in charge? We demand to know. We intend to hold them responsible: death would be too good for them. The search begins in the home, it begins just behind the mirror: there, in the bathroom cabinet, are the innocuous masters of our lives—the toothpaste, the deodorant, the shampoo. Someone has decreed that we should not remain during the days those briny, glistening starfish as which we crawled the bottoms of seas to suck up the smallest, reddest forms of life. It is not so bad to be in the air now, routine to live as two beings: one in the light, the other just beneath the light-tight skin of sleep. But to be the third thing: the creature that was given, by mistake, the demented brain, and now must absorb with flaccidity the daily dose of electricity that will prolong its self-knowledge. For it is one thing to be alive—the grass is alive, the pea and the potato grow, and microscopic algae stain with their living bodies the snow of the coldest regions—and another thing to *know* that one is alive. Where in philosophy was it decided that, if it is good to be able to choose, it is twice good to realize it? The argument that once raged inside the spiral corridors of a nautilus, at a depth a human being could only imagine, sings all around us like wind in the alleys, like city water in the sewers. We have not been shocked enough yet. We are not yet ready. Great areas of our brains still lie dormant like the liquid-carved underside of a coral reef. The debate rages in words and gestures. Sparks open up new hallways between logic and instinct. But it is in the dormant regions of the brain, the resonant cavities of absolute not-knowing, that life is closest to the source of life. A whole brain like that is like a head carried in on a plate. For a moment, it is one thing that looks like another thing. For a moment, everyone in the room could have sworn that it could see them, and that it blinked.

# Pulsations

One sees the trees ahead and the shadows underneath them
and feels the heat and humidity. One's foot throbs
like the body of a spider on the concrete sidewalk. One
has a thought or two, then torpor and the ache of fever.
One cannot express it. Yet one can know it completely.

One holds the hand of another in one's own, and sees
a shadow two make together, and sees the darker shadow
ahead, there where it is one is walking to, and the day is hot.
One's head dozes on one's neck even as one walks on.
One's eyes absorb the moist air and do their best to make pictures.

One has a thought about beforehand and another about afterwards.
Then torpor, and the padded planet sticks on its gear. One
goes among the leftover wrappers, the discarded dailies,
the bottle caps and beer tabs and other indications of humanity,
and sees among the litter the constant rearrangement of matter.

One moves oneself a few things about, slowly, surreptitiously.
There was a bird's egg nearly whole on the grass, and one
considered it to be perfectly flawed, its only fall from grace
the skylight through which the baby pecked its way free. One
thought how birds are so little bother considering their numbers.

# Poem in Orange Tones

Curtains hung closed, sealing off the window,
and the silver waste of a snail glistened
on the sidewalk outside, minutely rotting,
where night had taken its fluttering light away
and a rumbling in the world's belly
signaled the rising red of a day. Dew trembled
to keep its balance on a spear of grass.
Dirt lamented in the cemeteries. The fir
grieved not to be as hard as oak or olive.
Everything in the world regretted something—
the ash not to be fire, blue not to be red,
a radish not to have the smell of an onion.
Thus, with the whole world resisting waking up,
men and women, also, woke
slowly, reluctantly, with eyelashes melted together
and frozen brows
and would have tossed all day long in bed
like fallen leaves
if certain trees had not produced a sound like laughter,
if particular birds had not sung in orange tones,
or if the air had not wrecked itself
on the lower lip of the horizon. A white journey
was beginning, rosy in the distance,
a drone was starting to sound just under the surface
of the land, in the woods where it had been too wet
to echo and in the water, now that the moon
had stopped pulling
orphaned questions out of private prayers,
and it was time. The doors opened.
The curtains spread. What if there was to be rage
in the middle of metal, rebellion in some motor
somewhere, or wrath in the weather?
Whatever can happen will, and rakes will clatter
to clear the consequence of time,
and saws will sing to fell even the olive tree,
and the strength of the onion falter,
but still we live the days

as if in a crystal
in which the smell of fruit is increased
day by day by the sun.
And the color yellow regrets it was never green,
and the east and the west long to trade places,
and the shadow would like just once
to come out on top.

# Eastern Long Island

Beach grass tangled by wind—the sound rushes
to every nautical degree—
here are torn memories of inlets and canals,
of ponds, bays, creeks, coves, spits and sandbars,
coastal moons and skies, tidal clumps of tiny crabs
that couldn't keep up, seaweed fixed
to stones looking like the heads of Chinese sages,
all criss-crossing the sundial of my dreams.

I dream more when the meteors come—
Earth's face slipping through a comet's tail—
reminder that we steer an unmarked channel,
buoyless, sounding the vacancy of space
where water turns
to take back what it said and deposit on the shore
the exhausted sailor, his tired, complaining boat,
and the wrack of salt water pouring through the slats.

Wasn't anything to be done. Where ships foundered,
where pilgrims settled and pioneers set off,
now contaminant plumes propose
marriage to the aquifer, this being the way it was
when the shark lost teeth to the incoming tide,
and those legs that covet the tide line
were torn from the armored, methodical crab,
and the gull grabbed off the fish closest to the top.

Wasn't anything to be done—not then
when rapture simmered underwater, and we played
adulthood, taking sea horse and starfish,
nor later when the fishermen
followed their catch to deeper water,
leaving a stain that coated rocks and weeds
and seemed to be of a shade containing
its own shadow, an undulation in the channel.

Time has not ended. Yet already it is a struggle
to brush away the first few flecks
starlight lent this crystalline surface, then mute.
Earth's voice, a harmony begun in molten rumble,
rose through wash of water and rush of air
to the high pitch of grass blade and ether light.
Those first bits of impurity, that were to ruin
our diamond in the making, at first barely marked it.

I still love the radiance of a dim storm building
out where the tide seems to reverse and the sea vibrate,
puzzling perhaps to fresh eyes yet unfazed
by salt wells rising beneath these beds of clay.
At the tide line a fringe of seaweed keeps time,
and wind-whipped sand opaques our cottage windows.
By the boat ramp, disgorged clam shells await
reclamation by the proximate meek, who shall inherit.

# Ten Thousand Questions Answered

## 1. *Watching an Orange Moon Rise over Port Townsend Bay*

It is close, large, moving up rapidly.
And it rises where Mount Rainier stood in the light.
For a moment it rests on the summit of an unseen mountain.
A pinprick of light in the sky passes behind it.
So-and-so, the poet, says four lines in a stanza are too few.

## 2. *To a Pipefish Washed Up on the Beach*

Lying in mud, you escaped the life of bait.
The destiny of the pipefish—shiny, slender, electric—
is to become an offering to a larger catch.
Therefore, you lived longer by dying slowly.

## 3. *Sadness and Poetry*

Nothing is sadder than a book of poetry.
Before the book is begun, no sadness.
After the first poem, before the final poem—
there is no sadness before a thing is finished.
But afterwards, one grieves for one's failure.
The answer is to let the poem be too long to finish.

# Ecstasy

And there are cries, muffled, from a closed room,
and there is that kind of rough argument
that sounds like the tussling of a tiger and a stuffed bear,
and there is, in the moist lines of a lover's hand,
a narrative of need and desire
and the brief story of two who meet and instantly
know the full measure of their breathing,
each enlarged by the other's,
until the door falls open to let out the old cries,
and the argument is overcome by one ravaging swipe
of the tiger's claws, and they are set loose.

All the sorrow in the world
attends the bed where two find happiness,
and they will rise to it, bleached and drained, afterwards,
but now there are only legs like none other,
and hands and mouths like never before, and sensations
impossible before this moment, this dream.
In this feverish circle, which moves and does not move
at once, in this updraft of overweening feeling,
in this constant approach to the cliff
of afterwards, the lovers burn with reality,
and are emptied of it, and say they are happy.

There are natural limits to what may be known
about another, and the testing of it
is scored at night in the pipelines of tenements,
in vibrations on the surface of pooled water,
and in the personal thermostats of comfort
by those who close or open their eyes without blinking,
by those who toss and turn without restlessness,
and by those who shiver in fever and burn in cold.
You don't want to know this, unless you are so engaged,
how the lover craves more, openly,
how the lovers glue themselves together to be broken.

Without words, everything may be known at once.
Sing or scream, be light or heavy,
be utterly aware from the adrenaline of her desire
or dizzy from the accumulations of surrender,
you will feel it in the protruding parts of the body
as always, but then, if this is to be the true wreckage,
you will feel it in the in-turning areas,
there at the waist, in the creases and hollows,
at the neck, at the hinges of the wrist and knee,
in the curled-up sole of each foot, under
the drawn-in tongue, behind the lips, and in a line

that passes through the solar plexus. Explode now,
you are the world, you did not do this alone.
Bite your life in two, let the high frequencies
of your screams speak for you and the low level
of your moaning be the planet's undercurrent.
These are life, what you must come back to,
though it be closeted in public
as if it were to be doubted, or feared.
In bed, in arousal, in a savage sensitivity,
there the high fury of lovers feels eternal
as they fall and fall through the spray into now.

When it is over, you may strangle the bedside flowers.
When it is over, you may cut through the web
of that spider whom you protected and observed
at the doorway—for now is the cold at the window.
Akimbo, the lovers find themselves. Akimbo,
spun out from the center, cast nerve lengths
from that red coal withdrawing in the fire pit
which a thundershower has doused—
akimbo, the lovers gather themselves now
for the long climb up from the chasm. Others
said it was a human sacrifice—their friends come

to a perilous edge, and indeed a volcanic cauldron
simmered at the base. They themselves
simmered and burned and simmered some more,
and cooled, and now the climb needs handholds,
and one hoists oneself by tiny purchases
in sheets and coverlets, pushing off from the resistance
of aching springs and loosened headboards,
shaking free of a dampness, making for the high edge
where one first viewed the chaos like a visitor.
At the bluff, the high weeds have wilted,
exposing the beaten squares where blankets lay.

Dizzily, we look back and step away. Dizzily, we surge
out of the beloved, pushing aside our embrace,
and twist to see beyond a shoulder if any remain
of the last sparks and fire trails, whatever they were
at the base of the brain. Already nothing may be left
but a murmur of residual warmth as it rises,
like us, to mix with the hours an odd lightheadedness,
the source of which eludes and eludes us
as we dress again and concentrate on the days ahead.
Walk, now, as far as you like on shaky legs.
This place you found is not a room and has no exit.

How many plan to die while making love
and pay into every wishing well that the days ahead
resemble the past, that once, that burned? Confess,
student of smell, scholar of the kinetic nuance,
confess that, among all the creatures of the world,
men and women alone must thrash or resist
to reach pure feeling. And there are middles to stories,
and there are insects that click by, and flies
that simmer as they die in the candy of the spiderweb,
suspended, and there is the moment when the lovers
rip into the silence, to quiet it with their cries.

# Short Version of Ecstasy

Up-welling of forces, serums and fevers,
tracking conduits of emotion,
following the longing of waist, elbows and knees
to crease to and fro, to be wind and wild
as any petal of in-growing rose bud in storm.
Until, and not until, each still quivering tendon
flops its last and pales;
until, and not until, something of a trance or sleep
blankets the bed; until, and not until, a dozen instances
lift and collapse in a headless consciousness
of release, and the gorged blood descends
by an intermittent elevator of stems,
will the lovers let go of themselves or each other.

Can they stand to get up now? So far have they slid
from the inflated lungs of love,
from the gasping expectation and the drag
of skin on skin as they sank after having held up
their coming, they who moved as one
raw from the separate rates of their falling,
such a distance have they gone, up and down then,
that each may recall the middle of the story
only by its frame. After the event,
the photo of the lover expels no scent, no invitation
sufficient to satisfy. It is truly over until,
and only until, some hidden residue of passion
sways into being, wanting to die.

# Cryptic Version of Ecstasy

To have been a rose among white poppies,
to have opened to the delirium
that each day shatters the night on all sides
and at night pulls down upon itself the day,
and to have scrubbed the dripping wall
from the inside out, writhing with the labors
of harsh pleasure, to have felt one might
surely burst without again catching one's life
as it rose and dipped and vanished—
is to have been wooed and won.

And to have had a place to be streaming,
to have ridden the tossing vacancies
that lend the days their view from above
and the nights their plummeting echoes,
and to have turned the misshapen rod
from the outside in, pressing with the effort
of rough elation, to have known the moment
when the blooming occurs, like blood
among porcelain figurines—such is the prize
of true love, or so it was given me to say.

# Poem after Carlos Drummond de Andrade

*"It's life, Carlos."*

It's life that is hard: waking, sleeping, eating, loving, working and
   dying are easy.
It's life that suddenly fills both ears with the sound of that
   symphony that forces your pulse to race and swells your heart
   near to bursting.
It's life, not listening, that stretches your neck and opens your eyes
   and brings you into the worst weather of the winter to arrive
   once more at the house where love seemed to be in the air.

And it's life, just life, that makes you breathe deeply, in the air that
   is filled with wood smoke and the dust of the factory, because
   you hurried, and now your lungs heave and fall with the
   nervous excitement of a leaf in spring breezes, though it is
   winter and you are swallowing the dirt of the town.
It isn't death when you suffer, it isn't death when you miss each
   other and hurt for it, when you complain that isn't death,
   when you fight with those you love, when you misunder-
   stand, when one line in a letter or one remark in person ties
   one of you in knots, when the end seems near, when you
   think you will die, when you wish you were already
   dead—none of that is death.
It's life, after all, that brings you a pain in the foot and a pain in the
   hand, a sore throat, a broken heart, a cracked back, a torn
   gut, a hole in your abdomen, an irritated stomach, a swollen
   gland, a growth, a fever, a cough, a hiccup, a sneeze, a
   bursting blood vessel in the temple.
It's life, not nerve ends, that puts the heartache on a pedestal
   and worships it.
It's life, and you can't escape it. It's life, and you asked for it. It's
   life, and you won't be consumed by passion, you won't be
   destroyed by self-destruction, you won't avoid it by abstinence,
   you won't manage it by moderation, because it's life—life
   everywhere, life at all times—and so you won't be consumed by
   passion: you will be consumed by life.

It's life that will consume you in the end, but in the meantime . . .
It's life that will eat you alive, but for now . . .
It's life that calls you to the street where the wood smoke hangs,
    and the bare hint of a whisper of your name, but before you
    go . . .

Too late: Life got its tentacles around you, its hooks into your
    heart, and suddenly you come awake as if for the first time,
    and you are standing in a part of the town where the air is
    sweet—your face flushed, your chest thumping, your
    stomach a planet, your heart a planet, your every organ a
    separate planet, all of it of a piece though the pieces turn
    separately, O silent indications of the inevitable, as among
    the natural restraints of winter and good sense, life blows you
    apart in her arms.

# Just a Moment—I Am Busy Being a Man

Just a moment—I am busy being the brain of a man.
Just a moment—no colors, please, no sounds.
A little spittle being ground into dust, but no more.

Just a moment—I am busy being the heart of a man.
Just a moment—no thoughts, no politics please.
A little blood turned into pebbles, but it's enough.

Just a moment—I am busy being the soul of a man.
Just give me a moment—no aches and pains, please.
A minute alone with the corpse, one is plenty.

Being the brain, the heart and the soul of a man
isn't easy. There aren't any buttons, and no manuals,
and it's not easy—just a moment! just a moment!

# "PAGES"

O N the day following his sister's birthday, he takes up a position at the front window of the café. There he sits facing the street with his café au lait, two books, a pencil, a pen that writes intermittently, and a sheet of paper folded so that he might categorize his thoughts. At first he notices little that passes outside. Instead, he reads and sometimes writes. The reading stimulates him. More than that, it gives him solace and privacy. Between him and the author of the book he is reading, there is complete understanding. The solace of understanding and the security of privacy. A man alone with his thoughts, yet hardly alone at all. He begins to look up. A local artist, whom earlier he saw exiting the coffee shop and walking away, reappears on the far side of the street carrying wrapped flowers and walking briskly. Down an elevator in the sidewalk, a man delivers cases of beer. The temperature sign on the bank reads 33°. Afterwards, walking downhill in a light rain, he holds his hand in front of his chest so that the top of his unopened umbrella supports his chin. He is still thinking, lost in the utter security of the impermanent mind, oblivious to death as only a thought can be. The mind is not the brain. In any case, he rarely opens his umbrella, since the image of a man holding an open umbrella has always seemed to him silly. A man holding the string of a balloon or a parachute. A man trying to close an umbrella in the wind. Of course, he dresses informally and has no fear of getting wet. He carries only enough to put under his shirt in the rain. Hence, he is not a fair judge of the seriousness of the lives of other prisoners, nor of the effectiveness of umbrellas.

A R R I V I N G at the dentist's office, he is only two minutes late, so he is surprised to see two others in the waiting room and several coats hung from the hat tree. He takes a magazine and sits down to wait. When the receptionist appears, she greets him as if they were merely passing on the street. As if she expects him to explain himself for lingering. He only says hello and returns to his reading. But she says he must have made a mistake, his appointment is for later that day. That makes no sense to him. He has the appointment written down in three places. Suddenly he remembers. I know what it is, he says, I have a haircut appointment! He leaves the waiting room in a good humor and runs to his barber. When he explains why he is late, the barber says, Well, you knew it was something above the neck.

J A N E ' S Gift of an Apple. The sweet apple I didn't eat that day became the even sweeter apple I wouldn't eat any day. A year later, it has shrunk to half its original size, the red skin now pinched-up all about it, its color the brown of milk chocolate. A whiskey smell up close. An intoxicating idea at a distance: to keep something beyond its time is somehow to have kept it forever. No way now to throw it out. The shrunken, fermented apple is not a version of the apple it was. It is another thing, to another purpose. I myself am a version of all that I could never, not in a million years, have imagined I would become.

T H E Question of the Thirteenth. Where is Feb. 13? He flies out of San Francisco the day before and arrives in Sydney the day after. The 13th occurs for an hour and ten minutes during which passengers are permitted to deplane in Honolulu—where there is time again. Time hardly exists in a 747 flying over the Pacific in the middle of the night. At first the passengers try to keep a hold on time. The evening is marked off by: (1) drinks; (2) dinner; (3) a movie. But finally the cabin is dark and seemingly desolate. The passengers have ducked down to sleep across vacant seats. The attendants have disappeared into small closets of light, curtained off from the rest of the cabin, to read newspapers and "be available." The sense of time, along with the sense of location, fades. By Honolulu, time cannot be recaptured except by wakefulness and the faces of public clocks. The airline continues to insist that the layover is for refueling and to let some passengers leave and others join up. But we who are in the middle of longer flight believe we have been landed to return us to a sense of reality—"feet on the ground," etc.

We are told to remain in "the holding area." Isn't this proof enough that there are official fears for our sanity, our grasp of reality? We are permitted to exit the terminal only to the sidewalk that runs by the glass doors and walls of "the holding area." Therefore, most of us spend the time walking rapidly from one end of the windows to the other and back, and again to the far reach of our allotted path and back, etc. We walk faster than the short walkway requires. We are out of synch with the usual relationship of time and distance. We see the distance as a receptacle which we now are trying our best to stuff with time. We are ourselves filled only with distance, but we cannot understand it except in terms of time, which we barely recognize here, now, and which has lost for us its elasticity.

T H E morning newspaper arrives under his hotel room door at 4:45 A.M. Today's horoscope reads, "You will be concerned about something, possibly a small animal."

A bas-relief on a wall in the Botanical Garden, Sydney:

## TO THE HORSES OF THE
## DESERT MOUNTED CORPS

Erected by Members of
the Desert Mountain
Corps and Friends
to the Gallant Horses
Who Carried Them
over Sinai Desert
into Palestine
1915–1918

They suffered wounds,
thirst, hunger and
weariness almost
beyond endurance
but never failed
They did not come home
We will never
forget them

The boys in their school uniforms. The smallest of them carry the largest packs: little hunchbacks, bowed under the weight of learning. If it's learning. The government wants to begin charging tuition, the income to be used to increase course offerings in the areas of greatest demand. The academics are against it: they hold to the belief that tuition-free education is an incentive for the lower classes. But their opponents point out that university educations have remained the province of what is here referred to as "the middle class." It *is* the "middle class," all right: it lives in small houses in the suburbs and eats tiny sandwiches for lunch. It obeys the rules. But that same middle class is so far above the lower class in privilege, security, and rank that it might as well be called the "higher class." Those who are richer by far? They might be called the "world class," as the best athletes are, or perhaps "international class," since they travel, spend, and speak in many languages.

The girls in their school uniforms, separate from the boys.

90

T H E Australian love of city fountains is limitless. A tour could be made exclusively of Sydney's fountains. A week could be used up visiting the fountains and park statuary. Having sat by Sydney's fountains—many of them large, most of them encompassing some sort of cascading waterfall on all sides—Australia's other cities, even those set on the coast, seem landlocked. Sydney is water. Other Australian cities are merely *near* water. But then one comes to the National Art Gallery in Melbourne. It is closed, this being Monday, but one is drawn anyway to the great plates of glass at the front of the building. Water is washing down their length and breadth from above. A thin layer of water unfolds from top to bottom, continuously. One first assumes the water is falling on the inside of the window but, no, it is on the outside. Fill your hands with it. It is real. The lobby of the art gallery shows through the watery glass like a dream image. In a dream, everything is true. This is a brilliant fountain and waterfall, but it is also a brilliant window: one would not stay so long at an ordinary window, through which reality is apparent, clear, fixed, and dismissable. Here, one stays and stays, figuring out the physical nature of things, trying to solve the fluid mechanics of the thing, apprehending the nature of things inside as filtered through the ever-changing optics of watery glass panes. This is true poetic imagery: the thing itself transmitted through the imagination: transformed by subjectivity yet recognizable as external form. A chair is a chair. A Van Gogh chair is a Van Gogh chair. I stand by this window a long while, scooping occasional handfuls of water from the glass, using my fingers to deflect the water that clings to the surface of the window, altering the scene on the other side. The magical is shadowy. This must be the coolest spot in all Melbourne. City of sophistication, that felt challenged by the winged Opera House of Sydney, your best public moment is this children's plaything, this sloppy gravity-defying water-mirror, an enchantment of suspense and surface tension, cool sex, wall-walking, something we can't quite get at: hence, something pure.

The next day, a museum guard explains that it is done to cool the building and reminds him that this was once a common practice in butcher shops along with sawdust floors and animals out back.

A T A dinner party. A serious man who has said little all evening accompanies me into the library to see the bookshelves built and painted by our host. It is a large library. Most of the books, as in all huge personal libraries, are in perfect condition: unripped jackets, firm spines, etc. I mention that I have begun to get rid of books, recently selling seventeen cartons of books to a used-books store. "It was only a dent," I say, with regret. The serious man then tells me that his father sold off a large personal library to follow him to Australia. After that, he says, his father seemed diminished. His father was never the same again, in the son's eyes. The library had been such a big part of his father, he says. His respect for his father was shattered. He tells this as if it indicates his love of learning, his respect for culture, his intellectual engagement with life. To me, the story indicates only the crimes of culture. Someone should tell people what reading is and how writing occurs. Someone is. So many, however, use it to prop themselves up. Naturally, their fall is greater.

At a dinner party. We go out to look up at the Southern Cross. An extra star, faint, appears within the Cross. It is moving, yes, steadily. We realize that we are seeing a satellite spinning around the earth.

F O R months he has hurt during long walks. He assumes it to be a pulled muscle, and he finds that he can accommodate the pain by pressing the flat of his right hand against an area of his body just above his groin. He hooks a thumb over his belt and presses in on himself while he walks, looking on city streets like a man of power, wealth, or danger.

He doesn't realize he has developed a hernia. The bowel is pushing through a tear in the muscle. A "regular hernia," the doctor tells him, explaining the congenital nature of the weakness in the now torn muscle wall. She is matter-of-fact, and so is he. It is not difficult for him to go to a woman doctor with such an injury. If he were much younger, it might be. She sends him to a surgeon to make sure the operation can wait until his travels end. The surgeon is a man, but he is more feminine than the first doctor. The operation can wait. If the pain gets bad, he is to press the bowel back in through the torn muscle. Knowing it is not an emergency, and that he has all along been doing instinctively what can be done, he already walks better. Once in a while, he presses himself in while walking or sitting or lying in bed. Such is contemporary medical practice. He is hoping for a local anesthetic only. He has made sure that it is not necessary to "restrict sexual activity." It isn't, the surgeon smiles. In the meantime, he walks the streets of Australian capitals literally holding in his own guts.

INTERVIEW

Do you believe that actors are dumb? Writers?

Which of the following do you think are the dumbest: actors, writers, policemen, firemen, hunters, or generals?

How about social workers, teachers, doctors, realtors?

Fat people, prisoners, the poorly dressed, the visibly impoverished?

The sick, the old, the lovesick, the lonely; those who make mistakes in public, those who apologize, the silent, the talkative?

Do you approve of torture under any circumstances? Which?

What form of torture do you favor—physical, psychological, etc.?

Do you approve or disapprove of euthanasia? For others? For yourself?

What form of euthanasia do you prefer? For others? For yourself? Is cost an issue? Would you prefer that your death be carried out by someone other than yourself? Close friends? Family members? If a doctor shows up bearing a lethal injection, would you feel it improper to refuse?

Which bodily functions do you find the most embarrassing to discuss?

Are there things you would say to one sex but not to the other?

E X P L A I N I N G his typewriter. He explains that he has brought along a travel typewriter that he bought years before from J. H., who earlier published a long piece in *Life* on the poet John Berryman. Berryman was pictured in Ireland sporting a long gray beard grown abroad. He liked that article enough to save it. Now, he thought, could my typewriter be the very one on which she wrote so well of Berryman? He telephoned her, perhaps too early in the morning. But she was pleasant. Could it be? "Well," she said, "I had that typewriter then. It may be that it was. Yes, let's say that it was." Now, *he* says that it was, but then he tells the story also. Sometimes he goes straight to the story. Life is not a list of events but a continuum, yet he would have to live in a rain forest alone not to see his own life as a series of events in a context, a continuum, called Life. These events happen quickly—a few minutes now and then, even if they unfold in stages over years—but the stories that contain them surround them with Life. So after a while, rather than reporting an event, he tells the story of the event. The event passes beyond its normal boundaries. Also, it continues. Today, as he tells again the story of his typewriter, he is once more experiencing the question, Could it be?, and again the special answer in between yes and no ("Let's say that it was"), and again the delight in having one's cake and eating it too, in enlarging the events of Life without lying about them to oneself—and all of this once more for the first time. About his poems, C. was amazed, she said, by how he could make poems out of so little—"bits of string and thread, and some dust from under the bed."

T H E seminar. It is now possible to express the motives underlying this first journal seminar. A little honesty. First, the texts. Williams' *Paterson* now seems both brittle and spendthrift to me. The real genius of his long poem is the woman who addresses him as Dr. P. All that he is not, she is. She speaks of the grubby, prideful, self-deceived, careerist side of literature. Her needs bespeak the cruelty of the writer. His use of her letters bespeaks the utter cruelty of literature. I have noticed this.

# Pages #2

AUTHOR'S NOTE:

In the winter of 1986–87, while residing alone in a small house in the northwest, near a bluff above Port Townsend Bay, I kept a notebook of personal struggle not intended for publication. Sometimes, a page would begin in the language and feeling of a journal, move toward that of the essay, and finish in that of poetry. During the same period, I was compiling a *Selected Poems* and, as is my habit, obsessively rethinking matters of thought, emotion, and language. These pages are some that lingered there, whatever their true subject.

M. B.

T H E Journal of a Few Minutes to Midnight. Saturday, 13 Dec 86. First night in the house on Polk Street. Off the bluff, the gulls swoop and veer, taunting the old man who owns the big house at the edge with his earthiness, his mere flightlessness. Below, the car ferry makes its way in winter-roughened waters. Three sailboats have ventured forth but stay near shore. I understand both motives: the one that made these sailors take to choppy seas and the one that keeps them within easy reach of land. In the BayView, over breakfast, the local men at the next booth agreed that it was a foolish thing to sail out in the current weather. I have just driven three and a half days to reach this small port town on the tip of the Quimper Peninsula, which itself juts out from the better-known Olympic Peninsula. Here, in the far corner of the country, as far as one can go in the contiguous United States from the weight of literary power, I will live for eight months, beginning in the rainy season when the light fails at four in the afternoon and the night lasts sixteen hours. I love it here. For three to four months, the days will be windy and wet, and this town of six thousand, much of it unemployed, will live on its pennies until warmer weather brings in tourist dollars. And I will be counting my pennies, too, trying by sustained attention and solitude to determine for myself the value of my art.

D R E A M , night of 13 Dec 86. Two settings: Jason's room at school and some sort of literary festival. At the festival, an eager, self-confident poet insists on giving me a copy of his book—but only later, during the program. Somehow he walks off with the manuscript of my *New and Selected*. My only copy, held by one of those thick spring-bound binders (black) which double the weight of any project. I am off with Dorothy to see Jason in his room at the dormitory. When we arrive, he isn't in. His room is cluttered, but not so badly as at home. At the window, a radio is blaring rock music. I turn it down before I realize that in a courtyard below a dozen young men are playing catch. Now I understand that Jason's radio provides the music for this courtyard, and I move to turn up the volume, but now the station is different: soft melodies the young men below won't appreciate. I try to find the other station but can't. Then we are out of the room, walking through a large area (an empty parking lot?) toward the festival stage in the distance. I expect to find that the other poet has left his book and my manuscript for me, there on the surface of the lot. I do find a book and a black binder, but they are not intended for me. The binder is the *New and Selected Poems* of another poet, one well known to me, and the book too has been left for him. We go forward to sit near the stage. The poet shows up to read. He gives me his book and my manuscript and I am relieved. He is a poor poet but reads with great confidence. It quickly becomes clear that his gift was a way of forcing me to sit through his reading, nothing more. We leave quietly. As we are returning through the lot, a woman who holds up a sign like those at political conventions announces to late arrivals that there will soon be a session on sexual awareness, or some such subject. Whatever the title, I recognize a new form of touchie-feelie feel-good pop psychology, and it seems clear to me that this festival, the young poet, and much of the poetry scene has lost its muscles and brains to this warm oatmeal sense of what it is to be human. In Jason's room again, I see an M-1 rifle on a tripod. I am at first alarmed, but then I remember that all students must take R.O.T.C. I am even less bothered by the presence of this practice rifle when I see on his desk a crude set-up for hand-turning clay into small pots, and what appear to be pinkish lumps of clay.

I understand that his room shows his emerging independence and a modest confidence. When he arrives, I ask if it is an inconvenience to have a passage from the side of his room into the ceramics lab, which I can see down the hallway. He says no, though it makes it a little wet.

2 1 D E C 8 6. The question of what I am up to. I am carving my own face. I am taking responsibility for the furrows on the hillsides and the wheel marks in the grass. I am absorbing all the moisture of a northwest seaside winter. I am closing the walls of my feelings about the deep, insistent winds that ride the bluff. I am in the distance and at home, hurrying to move and hurrying not to move. I often write, now, some prose on a page of poetry, or some lines on a page of prose. Afterwards, I find I want to keep the lines of poetry and the paragraphs of prose together. There is something about the prose, the more so if it is journal-prose rather than prose-poetry—something (intimacy? the raw?) that lends specific gravity to the poetry. If the foundation of a poet's argument is shabby, a loud style and a skill-ful use of interval can distract the reader from basic considerations. Prose, however—at least the kind of journal-prose I am thinking of—is so properly and obviously the home of sustained attention and loyalty to argument that the poets of theory and willful imprecision must avoid it. In any case, the key to William Carlos Williams' "tri-adic stanza" is the sentence. The essence of the poetic sentence is the phrase as it holds hands with the line. And the secret that contains the poem made of sentences composed of phrases distributed in lines is just this: prose was always poetry. Today, prose has the greater freedom to be poetry, because poetry is the victim of its own con-ventions. Most poems today are written to sound like poems; hence, written according to vaguely understood, ill-defined conventions of theme, development, what constitutes a beginning of a poem, what constitutes an ending, how does a poem sound and proceed, etc. It would be a happier and more productive circumstance if poets tried to write bad poems, without being silly or nonsensical. For then every move made by the poet to make the poem less like other poems would only make the poem more and more interesting. One must constantly understand the hidden rules of poetry so as to better vio-late them. There is no hope for the numbers on the pages. And it is always the hottest day of the year for the globe of the world that sits on a table underneath a lamp. So much is the constant rain outdoors against the artificial suns inside. The white balls of light flood my plate and my page. If the intention of such circumstance is to keep

at least a few thoughts from leaving prematurely, then circumstance must be given its due, and the prose kept by the poetry to absorb much of the otherwise blinding light.

2 3  D E C  8 6. In the morning, I gather eight-inch pine cones with my bare hands—stupidly, because large, wet pine cones leave behind pine tar, applying it to one's hands in a spotting technique that depends completely on the aggression of those naked hands. In the afternoon, I am sitting in my car on the Hood Canal Bridge watching a submarine arrow its way through the opened bridge. It seems to drag its fin at a distance, and its conning tower reminds me of the smokestack of a squat locomotive. Men on the tower in orange life jackets. A hard wind causes the bridge to sway, the lamp poles to swing, and my small car to lean from side to side as if it had it in mind to dance. I have tuned in the news on the car radio. Sakharov, the Russian physicist, is back from internal exile. Voyager, a flying fuel tank, has made it round the world without stopping for gas. I feel that I have everything to love for as long as that may prove possible. But first it is necessary to wash my hands of pine tar, and I ruin a scouring pad in the process, and it will take two and a half hours to drain the broken water heater, by which time there will be music through the night easy to hear.

2 5 D E C 8 6. It's a yo-yo life at the end of one's fingertips. All bitterness (just an example) is of the emotions. It, and its raucous pals—good fellows all—live in the biology of the blood, in the chemistry of the body. The mind knows better. It can say, "I am angry," but it can also say, "I understand." Thought, I think, is of the electricity of the body, the binary jungle of the brain. Thoughts are not threatening. Censorship is not aimed at thought, although it *thinks* it is, but at the emotions. Mobs aren't a response to dialectics but to flags. My question: is it possible to live among emotions— a life at the end of one's fingertips—as one can live among one's thoughts, without the chemical extravagances of helplessness and cruelty? Surely it is a matter of conditioning and, too, of abandoning one's willfulness. When Williams writes that there is "only one solution: to write carelessly so that nothing that is not green will survive," he has caught on to the limitation, the fatal flaw, in willful aesthetics, in any theory of writing, in any method that claims to know good from bad, appropriate from inappropriate. I would go further, as the woman of *Paterson* does, the young Marcia Nardi who writes to "Doctor P." Her language simmers. Her whole being is pressed against the glass. Williams has it in him to be like her. In his secret life, he dances naked before the mirror in his north room. He would go further, but he is not in a position to. He cannot fall far enough. He cannot fall at all. To live more in the emotions is to fall. One must literally take on weight. The ethereal life of the brain, with its vain assertions of purity, is like water on all sides. It looks as if one could simply step through, but the surface tension is very great. If anyone can break through so thick a glassy wall, there will be a flood made up of unrehearsed emotion, a cascading greater than Niagara's, on which one's being must drop to the very bottom of a gorge before a single thought can intervene. Williams instinctively knew the power of the falls, central to *Paterson. Paterson* without the falls is a silly metaphor for critics. If Williams could only have been that young woman, and himself as well! He wanted to be. He came as close as he could to the idea, incorporating her letters into the body of his poem, making her a part of the dance of his poetry. Now I would apply his discovery to the emotions: only one solution:

to feel (live) carelessly so that nothing that is not life-giving will sur-vive. It takes a certain helplessness. It takes a fall. And sometimes there is no music present to put a limit on solitude.

2 5–2 6  D E C  8 6. Journal of the Perverse Nature of Ice. Watch for it, says the sign next to the highway, "Watch for Ice." That's black ice, those otherwise glassy irregular shapes that look like shadows on the black roadway during the day. Now, it is necessary to note that many have traveled the line to reach the paragraph, but it is rare that anyone successfully travels the paragraph to reach the line. The novelist who ends up as a poet began as a poet. It is at least as necessary now to establish the difference between loving and believing in. In the middle of a busy street, against the traffic, a young woman stopped to say that she was unable to decide which she wanted most: to be loved or to know the truth. For the moment, she wanted only orgasm and repose. As for the truth . . . as another woman said to me during a walk in the woods, "There are people who get it, and there are people who don't." The first of these became an experimental prose-poet of delightful, yet frivolous, sensuality. The second became a formalist whose meters and rhymes served with great skill the poetic conventions of intellectual detail and regret. I loved her for her laugh, not for her sense of humor. Thus, it may be worth noting that the headlights of an approaching car as it climbs a hill under a fog only slightly risen above the roadway light up the mist with an angelic glow, as if a pocket of illumination were soon to descend to earth, bearing belief and love, arriving like lightning inside a white cloud. And across the long, low stretch of the bridge on the Hood Canal, one day turns into another on the clock, and the first news of the day leaves a series of accidents in the air.

3 0  D E C  8 6. Journal of a Drive. Leaving Port Townsend, driving south in sunshine, I enter a fog in a matter of only a few miles. After that, it is alternately sunny and foggy. Where fog hangs above the road, the sun comes out of the east to pass its light through tall pines which literally separate and array it across the highway. The image is good enough to make one feel religious. I feel at such times as if one's life—one's entire lifetime—need come to nothing more than that one should see these magnificent and temporary performances of the planet. I remember a friend crying in the sight of the Oregon coastline, saying, "I don't deserve to see this." Along the narrow state highway by which I begin the journey from one peninsula to the other, a driver has stopped to turn left where a truck is parked on the shoulder to his right. Already, as I approach from a distance, several cars have stopped in back of him to wait. I sense that the line is already too long, that one of the drivers behind me will not understand the image: the line of cars ahead will seem too long to be standing still. As I squeeze past the one with its turn signal blinking, I stamp down on the accelerator pedal to get away. Even as I shoot ahead, I hear the crash. One car has hit another, a third has taken to the shoulder behind the truck. In the mirror, I can see that it wasn't anything to cause serious injury, and I keep going, blinking my headlights at approaching cars. Soon I am on the Hood Canal Bridge, enveloped once more by fog, squinting in the glare. I have never seen a glaring fog before, one that lies thickest at each side and concentrates what light gets through from above straight at you. Past the bridge, along clear roadway, there is a smoking stump. A tree stump six feet high, soggy with rain water and the foggy damp that has lifted, smokes in the sunshine. Perhaps because of the light that came through the high pines between the mountains and the road, I think of how important it is to the young poet to be seen as an experimenter, a discoverer of new forms, and how the need to surprise and amaze others gives way to the desire to tell the truth, and how no young poet should ever understand this beforehand. Then why am I now writing in what may be an unpublishable form: in between prose-poetry and the journal; in lines, then again not in lines; in pages of both lines and paragraphs. Is it because truth requires its own forms, and the truths I seek require a context larger than

the field of individual creation on which the poem is constructed? Is it that truth needs a logic beyond the usual small steps of imagistic association? Well, it is all too apparent during a drive that starts and ends in sunshine, journeys through fog, past accident, over a bridge beneath which one cannot see water, into and beyond mysterious and powerful combinations of leaf and light, with glances backward and thoughts ahead. It seems to hold meaning when a black sports car turns in front of me carrying a license plate that reads "terror." There is always a breeze around a candle, which is otherwise vulnerable without a shield—if only a generous hand cupped about it. So it has become for poetry, which has come to be in our day too easily chipped away at the edges without some prose to surround it. It is, of course, impractical to attempt to say the whole of the smallest idea, or to incorporate all that which touches upon a single, small, distinct subject. However, it may be possible to make certain suggestions, if one is not in too much of a hurry. The more so in fog. Even so, arrivals are much overrated.

J O U R N A L of the Second of January. As usual, the Quimper Peninsula gets more wind and less rain than that portion of the Olympic Peninsula just south of the Hood Canal Bridge. The wind here can make a gloomy day seem darker. Also, it spreads the edges of one's solitude. Solitude is a small, necessary business of the soul. It is centered, it has specific gravity, it stays in one place, which is why one may retain it in the midst of others and easily in the next room from the crowd. Loneliness is not that, but a large, gratuitous difficulty of the heart. It makes a grown man a loose reed in the wind, it has heaviness without weight, and it feels the worse for being so easily undone. The dark day and the hard wind and the leftover rainwater and the empty street and the quiet house let solitude be transmuted into loneliness if one lingers too long before doing the things that solitude improves. It seems to me that the true writer of journals is never in danger of true loneliness, yet the true writer of journals, more than others, seems to be reaching out, as if to another, as if out of utter aloneness. This notion is reinforced, perhaps, by the conventional notion that journals derive from women's diaries in which, we would have it, the writer is biding time while she waits to be rescued. It is merely a trick of literary form, which I much prefer to the tricks of language. Tricky language is lies. Tricky literary form is form. All the difference in the world. Do I write out of loneliness? I don't think so. Out of solitude. Surely. Not that I haven't tried to write at times to fill the time and to find a reader. But nothing of spirit ever came from it. The best that can be said for such periods is that they used up a time in which neurotic loneliness obstructed true solitude. I have always hated loneliness. I have likewise always enjoyed my solitude, even the idea of it. Colin Wilson's *The Outsider* and *Religion and the Rebel*, the jazz world of nighthawks, the just-emerging Beats, a few friends to the side of the law, Greenwich Village and Hyde Park (Chicago) in the fifties, the photography scene at the Institute of Design (Chicago) when Siskind and Callahan were the guts, little Alfred University with its Bauhaus-style Department of Design whose students would actually break into the Art Building at night to work, the Poetry Workshop in Iowa City when such programs were rare and still disreputable and the student writers likewise—these were the locations of my identity, or of that portion of it I would be permitted to create. A distinction should be made, or why did I not see my being a Jew, for example, as a source of my sense of myself? I didn't, that's all. It never occurred to me to. It was a method, a requirement, a handy factor in the course of philosophical attachments. But a source of identity? No. That, I apparently thought, I would fashion for myself. I have often said the obvious about the disproportionate role of minorities and the oppressed in creating the art of a nation, but I hesitated to apply it to myself so directly. How often we make alliances where we might have been expected to. I can't speak for others, but for myself—I wish to remain eccentric, but not in public.

12 JAN 87. I had forgotten, living for decades in a house with children, on a neighborhood street along a bus run, in a town of students and their renewable sources of energy, how much less sound there had been throughout my youth. Here, I am reminded. Nights, Polk Street suffers little interruption. My neighbor says she can sometimes hear the thump of the foundry at work at the edge of town. Once, three sonic booms in quick succession startled me into thinking that someone at the door was using his forearms to knock. Most of what one hears, however, is indoors, some of it in the inner ear. The jabbing sounds of rainwater falling from the roof and the rush of wind encircle the rooms of isolated light in which I am awake. Outside, I have heard the closed-lips hum of a float plane easing down into the bay by the boat yard, and the sizzle of the street light. And this night I must include the would-be voice of a clouded moon flat against Earth's shell of vapor. Inside, there is the nasal hum of electricity making heat and ice, the clucking of metal panels inside the baseboard heaters as they warm up at irregular intervals, the syncopated creaking of a hinge on a door left ajar. I know there to be the usual musketry and bee-sounds of the actual inner ear: source of dream imagery. In moments of whole quiet, the shell of my ear catches the full-wave sound of a universal ocean. For the rest, here is a resonant cavity, a chamber of indeterminate frequency, the body of a man temporarily inhabited.

In poetry, what is sometimes mistakenly called "silence" is, in fact, interval. Cage, attributing his sense of composition to a remark by Thoreau: "Music is continuous; only listening is intermittent." A silence that is not an interval will be available to all of us soon enough. We interrupt it with our lives. I would prefer a poetry that knows this without taking it for its subject. Give us the drone of death, and we will work enough variations in the higher notes to make you forget there was ever a night in which you were asleep.

Wrapped in the cold, now the clock in the courthouse tower lets loose its twelve solid bell tones—loud tonight, heavy tonight, falling with the weight of a hammer upon an anvil. The sound could be the clanking of a broken machine except for the music of it, made to ring out the emptiness of its shape.

Here's a jar to drop a pencil into, and again.

3 1  J A N  8 7 . The ceaseless wind of a day has blown down the beach grass, but a rose blooms on the calm side of the tree line. I continue to work best mornings just after rising and late nights, while the late afternoon as the light fails will do for willful beginnings that can be given their heads. Morning and late night—times closest to sleep and dreams. Time and no-time connected at both ends. Just so, rhetoric without sensory equivalents becomes the distortion of runaway grammar. The logic of it "makes sense," but the sense is wrong. Hence, the importance of the physical world in poetry, the lasting influence of imagery, the apparent sincerity of the story, etc. But the sentences that contain these things lie just because they are sentences. Nature is not a list, yet nature contains no prepositions, articles, conjunctions, and the like. What some people call "the irrational" must needs be placed among the rhetorically sound and the rational to complete the truth of life. Hence, the shine of the violin must accompany the dull sleeve of the musician as he saws a continuum of sound into portions of pitch and length. Adagio of thumbtacks. Andante of the slide rule. Allegro of the turning compass. No poem will stand up to the unprogrammatic in music unless it first soak itself in an unselective yet localized paste to which all adheres. For this, rain will suffice. Inside, the musicians tune up against the moisture in the air. Outside, crows and gulls stand in under eaves, hiking up their wings now and then without persuasion.

1 FEB 87. High tides, wind and rain have undercut two waterfront houses on Vashon Island. I often saw the same thing on the East Coast: on Fire Island, homes built on stilts to let the dunes move underneath, one day after a storm out in the water on their poles and the soft ground underneath them sinking lower. The concert pianist who survived certain death in a plane crash (broken back, severed aorta) returns to his music by way of Bach (unable to employ his pedal foot), saying that now he is most interested in "direct communication." There in a nutshell is the dilemma of experiment. Two things must go on at the same time—that which is experimental and that which is not—so that the experiment may go unnoticed. The conjunction "and" and its reverse "d-n-a" are a fair representation of the related and the discrete. Poetry has seen heavy labors to connect all things, to represent the universe, to mouth the sound that contains all other sounds, to calculate the transformation of thing into image, image into symbol and symbol into archetype. In conversation, we are able to look to the side and back again. We are able to follow the red thread of our words while we recognize other things to say which are not, existing as they do inside our minds, interruptions of the moment but whole components of it. The poem, so far exteriorized in the convention of the poetry reading, must retain for itself the irregular, the aside, those phrases and sentences which seem to be spare parts for other pieces. The selectivity of poetry has been identified with a "normal" range of association and logic, whereas sufficient force may, in time, extend the range of normalcy. The notion of "closure" has not been helpful. After the fact, in any case. Tie a knot in your lasso and see what you catch. Those people who got out just before the mud slid and the bank fell spoke to the camera as if they felt saved. Money can make you dumb, but not *that* dumb. Direct communication: alive or dead. Meanwhile, the lunch meat gets slippery, the milk thickens, yesterday's bread already blackening—just before the whole house falls to its knees before nature.

5 FEB 87. A bloodworm is drying out on the sidewalk while the sun is still low enough in the morning to throw its warmth from under the clouds that will block it most of the day. This date we count forty wars going on around the world. Liberace has died, and the disc jockey plays him singing, "I'll Be Seeing You." Schmaltz lingers, as probably it should. Someone thought poetry a young man's game— someone who would. Actually, he specified lyric poetry. Lyric poetry being, according to Aristotle, all poetry that is not epic (long narratives) or dramatic (verse plays)—when someone says "lyric poetry" he might as well just say "poetry." For if poetry is more than a vessel, more than a skill, more than a pattern broken only for effect, then it is the "lyric" poetry (using Aristotle's categories) that earns the designation "poetry" for such forms as the epic and the play: that is, the lyric poetry within story and dialogue.

So when it is said that poetry is a young person's art form, what is meant is that romance and sentiment are the province of the young, full of possibility, dreams, and the remnants of their innocence, which the grownup, of course, has replaced with likelihood, observation, and the continuous layering of experience.

Not so, I think. No doubt this seems true of the civic man and woman. They have a job to do, perhaps others to protect. They benefit by having teeth and showing them. But what happens inside? Everyone knows this. The knowledge of our ignorance overshadows the knowledge of our knowledge. Relativity replaces the absolute. Likelihood gives the lie to the notion of progress. Astronomy puts us in our place. Entropy, Malthusian theory, and the physics of the universe diminish the news of the day. What is left is romance. It may be a romance born of reality: likelihood reveals the futility of rational thought, especially if one's day-to-day survival seems assured; thus, one lives more and more in one's emotions, perhaps in secret, and even ideas are valued for the play of the emotions which intersect them. Or it may be a romance born of unreality (a grand or grandiloquent generalizing of the human condition; on the other side, those essentially hopeless enlistments in astrology, the reading of auras, channeling, and other such manifestations of easy authority).

Hence, a man may have a passionate feel for chess or Go. He may experience what life feels like in the golden-tinged circle of electric light at the bottom edge of a particularly graceful lamp shade or in the sphere of his daily errands. If all that could be said of a blood-worm stuck to the cold cement of a local morning were to be said, it would be enough. I am myself equally weary of the shouted emotion and the encoded emotion in poetry, both of them heavy favorites of our critical season. I am inclined to alter Lincoln's famous remark about the faces of men to say that nature gives a young poet his voice but by middle age he has made it what it is. A piece of glass should let the light through. I myself like to see through it as well. For everything on the other side is an elegy.

10 FEB 87. Journal of the Night of Blue Light. Pairs of three-second blasts from a foghorn separate the evening. Such a small town still that elementary school teachers bring their students to the post office to learn to mail a letter. The long line snakes past the bulletin board and up to the stamp window. I prefer this post office way of picking up one's mail at a box in the lobby to home delivery on someone else's schedule. Small-towner myself, I only regret that there is but one delivery—and that sorted by 9 A.M. Letters are the reason the woods quake when a highway is extended. Letters open the eyes of the mermaid nailed to the prow of the boat roughed up by distance. Well, one day when I was wondering if bird song would ever be my song, an old curse came to me: the curse of leaving. First, losing; then, leaving. I had it wrong when I thought that little losses are the forerunners of a final loss. In truth, losing is the preparation for leaving. We have trouble with the concept of leaving. Our language stops at the thought of death. Our sentences depend on an unending future. The vanity of clocks. So a letter gains importance as words left behind. In it, the past coils back around the present. As the years pass, one gives up without losing touch. The blue light of an evening is a curiosity one can hold in the globe of an eye. The shouts of the ship's horn can lie in the chamber of an ear like a sleeper who turns periodically in his sleep and, as he moves, smooths the sheet before him with his hand. Is it preposterous to liken these things to one another? Then the glass sea is preposterous and compassion impossible, and it is ridiculous to carve eyes in the head of a wooden mermaid. The lowest recorded temperature of all time is still something to write home about. Next to a thermometer, with its ruler of discipline, the face of a clock is a wheel of vain permission. I do not ask of a letter that it seem to suspend the passing of time, but only that it be aware that it has been sent to a future with the big hands of an Antarctica. Of all blues, it is the blue of ice that best matches the night.

1 5  F E B  8 7. Journal of the First Rainbow of the Year. Larry and I are standing near the cedars between our houses, talking about the sinister look of submarines, when a light rain moves us underneath a tree. A great rainbow arches from Point Hudson to Point Wilson. It appears in the only patch of blue sky in four directions and stands firmly for a few minutes until clouds erase it. It is the winter of El Niño: a warming ocean floor warms the water which in turn warms the air that is blown east. The warmth reaches all the way to the Midwest where it picks up a layer of the Great Lakes and turns it into snow for New England. But rainbows don't travel. Disparate, each appears and disappears in one location for its moment, however brief, as if to anoint that circumstance of elements and to empower those who have seen it to live in the mind of that moment when the moment has passed. In Marrakesh, we turned a corner and stopped. Something was wrong with our rented automobile, and we stopped and left it. And there over the edge of the city was a double rainbow. The double palette gripped in its curve the Moorish walls of gray and white, it gathered the dirt of the street and the smells of the animals, it stopped for a moment our indirection, and then it faded away. Such is the power of scarce pleasure. But there are places, tropical and near-tropical, where even rainbows are commonplace. Driving uphill through the Manoa Valley on Oahu, we passed through veil after veil of rainbow. From the ridge, looking toward the harbor, we sometimes wavered in our science, believing the ends of the optical arch of that morning bore particular addresses. In reality, rainbows are the reconstitutions of unrecorded time, the skyway fantasies of a young planet paying for water with heat. The myth of the phoenix as the fabled embodiment of Earthwater sucked up by the heat of the sun. The transcendence of the individual a flameout briefly signaled by a flurry of charged color somewhere above our heads—and gone.

1 5 FEB 8 7. Finally, I always feel more alive for writing, and writing in paragraphs goes on longer than writing in lines. Shall we call this an aesthetic? Tonight the light from the Navy refueling station on Indian Island is pinned against a low strip of cloud. The moon is white-faced to be seen through those thin fabrics that make the sun's light seem to stream away to reach people. It is not true. The moon hasn't cried since 1954. All the long tears of its defeat have fallen into places no one now remembers or would understand. The moon was the invincible cache of our romance.

U N D A T E D Pages. Already (three days) the manuscript so many years in the making seems far away and lifeless to him. He means it: lifeless! First, one's children are always home. Next, they leave occasionally. By seventeen, they are seldom home when anyone else is awake. Still it seems as if they are there—tangibly present—when they are not. But let them leave, actually move their bed and board, even to the other side of the same small town, and they are as gone as a stone thrown into a river, the memory of them as wistful and hopeless as a brilliant musical chord disassembling in the wind. How new our lives are when we are left with only ourselves—those of us of whom intimacy has produced one person where there were two to begin. How we struggle to regain the old life. We would, if the truth be known, crush the spark that took them from us if we could have them back. We would gladly live in the ashes of the house that burned. Not to do so will take the effort of an Houdini under water wearing a strait jacket, but it will not be a trick. It will be a birth— a bloody, unlovable birth defying the laws of hygiene.

Pages # 3

A dream. A poet whom I like appears to like me as well, but there is a question in my mind as to whether or not this is intentional. The poet's wife and I in a car. She driving. We talk of the distinctive style of her husband's poems. I refer to some characteristic of the lines. "Well," she says, "those are Bill's stanchions." She and I agree that the sky is constantly coming into Bill's poems. I mention that he is a poet of skulls. The telephone rings to end my dream, but not before I become aware that, in saying Bill is a poet of skulls, I have hit upon something.

## To the White Page

By the lilacs, hunched for winter, a transparent globe
hangs empty—that previous to these months was a world.
A world of sugar water to hummingbirds, who stood to eat.
Here and there on the grass a red or blue flower
and over there under the big tree a carpet of pine cones
stuck in the grass that erupted in random clumps
after the last cutting. The sound of a baritone horn
rides inside the night wind and shakes the hollow feeder:
"Wake up, don't sleep so deeply, don't give up!
Elsewhere a bird is conducting itself with still fury
and will return to you. The world is not, not empty."

I write in the dark, late at night, after long lethargy. Since I was a boy, I have liked to stay up after others, working in this or that private world. When I say that I write "in the dark," of course I mean the darkness of half a world. Inside, I prefer plenty of light—not the elegance of carefully placed spots of light, but an extravagance of light that reaches the corners, light that can carry the sound of a flute as well as the bark of a tuba. I walk about my rooms, sit at my table, and work against the night and the relative silence of post-midnight "out there"—and against sleep. I welcome the burning sensation on the surface of my eyeballs which begins at one or two A.M. I pull my shirtsleeves down as the room grows colder. I flex my fingers through their stiffness. I lower my head and swing it from side to side to restore the muscles of my neck. And then little or nothing is left of the demands of will to prevent the opening up of the skull. Images of feeling shake free of their origins to line up in the matrix of an idea which did not exist during the earlier part of the evening. This goes on until a limit has been reached, by which time I am without words and can barely make it into bed. I have succeeded in stamping out my mind. In the morning, the evidence of the page smells like a baby.

## 8/2/87

He stood before a sea of envelopes,
as others stand over a plunging surf.
One by one he began to open them,
to read the letters inside.
Since he had no hope of replying,
he pictured them adrift in the distance.
Free to walk by the water, he did.
He saw the wild ducks, far out specks,
dip their necks and drown awhile
for food, then alive again elsewhere!

Meditation on Kicking Over the Traces. I am disappointed to see
that my tracks remain on the beach. Returning the way I came,
I do not think of Crusoe's man Friday or of a path recovered.
I walked out low on the beach, edging the low tide, impressing
the mud—a sop to ignorance. I regret the wisdom in each step I
recognize as I double back. I stop to crack a washed-up spine and
to shuffle a pool's worth of tiny stones. All the while, I advance
by breathing, raising and lowering my iron stomach, blaspheming
the unsure footing as I twist and retwist ankles ruined by fool-
ishness, tendons torn from leg bones on playing fields devoid of
rain. I open and close my arthritic hands, which otherwise hang
half-cupped. I make a fist with my left hand and swing a slow over-
the-shoulder roundhouse to unhitch a cranky elbow. As always, I
borrow a stone to carry.

Another silent period broken. White glue. The time in between stretches of writing takes many forms. An anthology of one-line poems. Titles without lines. Phrases of light that go out for lack of a connection. A sky that celebrates the anniversary of a previous sky. A valveless brass instrument on which one may sound no more than the fragmentary call of a single bugle. Although I suffer writing blocks, I do not believe in them. No, blocked writing is not this loss of language. I suffer *value* blocks. I write to undo or evade the specious and to find the forms for values. Thus, my "writing blocks" are places where the path goes under the brush, where my thinking dead-ends for a while. I have run out of form, or I have run out of values: the consequences are the same. In any case, the numbers remain in the flat land of the wristwatch until writing recommences. Then it explodes, and time is scattered to the vast corners of the universe. I am up all night riding my spine, a witness to the hard moan of the black wind and the serial whiteouts on the far side of exhaustion. It is the winter of this winter, when every so often a homeless man will burn to death from sleeping too close to the fire. Periodic news fit for a bugle. As for philosophy, it was simple when we had nothing. It is some reassurance that we are alone.

## Your Vision or Mine?

Let's say for the stars they signal a heartbeat.
Let's say for the moon—a representative, a face.
The intervals, space—that's ignorance.
Meanwhile—meanwhile—
here a heart pulses like a burning star,
throbs beneath a face drained of its color.
Code Blue—behind the curtain, they work on him
where he fell a long time to try to reach a room.


## A Hundred Words

A young editor calls to ask if I will read a book
of poems—all about sailing!
I look out my window over the bluff to the bay.
No sailboats today. An anchored freighter.
a back-and-forth car ferry, a tug and a barge.
Choppy water. A string of logs for the paper mill.
Do I not love the first hundred yards, a hundred words?

It is Undershirt Day across the street. Six of them fly in the wind, lightly held to the line by pins. They have speed in one place. They are the easy, casual, weekly, domestic cousins to the still point of a turning circle. Kicked back from the rope by strong wind and held suspended, they give off the exhilarated anticipation, the spring-loaded power, of young swimmers just before the gun. Released, they would crumple among the frizzy limbs of bushes that mark these streets in the windy season. Held, they look as if they might reach the courthouse two blocks away where the wind tears at a mammoth American flag, making and remaking it with the flapping sound of a furious chambermaid. Well, these things are only and completely themselves. Every metaphor, every comparison, every notable parallel are the accomplishments of regret. One wants to be filled by things as they are, and, when this occurs, to tell others. For ultimately, things as they are do not require the worst actions of men and women. But things as they are are rarely seen as they are, and poets must admit to their role in transforming reality. Indeed, there are those who value literature for doing just this: transforming reality, which they find unacceptable, into phony compliments to possibility. Thus, Actress Fruitcake is coming to town to give instruction, for a fee, in "energy balancing," "getting in touch with one's past lives," etc. There will be no peace in a world of bliss-ninnies. Given up on this world? Then it is handy to believe in another. I myself prefer the belief that hangs six white undershirts on the clothesline once a week, wind or no wind. And tomorrow will be Underpants Day.

Dark clouds of the north.
Sky rides on the surface of the canal.
I speed past Shine Road and Paradise Road.
The orange cone of the buoy.
Sunbreaks. The sun runs behind the pine trees:
visual equivalent to a stick run along a picket fence.
I am following a path of hidden forces

through the shadows cast by overpasses,
long in the rapture and futility of highways.
A sky that was chronic
turns into a measure of distance.
The blue that was a boy's favorite,
that should have faded in time, takes back the sky.
I am the boy who has been waiting for the sun to come out.
I will always be the boy who is waiting.

## To Pain

We share a sun, a moon, heavens of stars.
We ride the same light into the forest.
The leaves have fallen before winter.
A few corpses lie where they were caught
in the forks of trees. The rounded
wish of a kerchief or a watch cap is our spring.
My corduroys, knee-worn, let more in now.
The dew that was is snow. I have the family
hands—arthritic. I open and close them.
I open and close and open them.
The wind whispers, and the leaves sigh.

What we do today is hard-won though it be only the drinking of
a cup of tea by the window and a steady look at the light in the
trees. What we do today will be daring though it be the slow walk
of an errand. What we do today will be new though it happen on a
local street. And the fate of the world will once again extend from
each small act of ordinary witness. I do not wish I had known
then what I know now. To the contrary, I hope to know now what
I knew then. In the Journal of Unified Light, there is a page on
which to record the moment at which the day begins: a registry
of birth.

*Page*: Conference on "The Individual and the Community"

A: During a lecture, the speaker says "the silence of magic" instead of what he meant to say: "the silence of marriage."

B: At the Conference. It is now possible to write down the rules: (1) The more "interdisciplinary" a paper, the more gobbledygook it will contain; (2) The more interesting the setting of a conference (as here, on the coast, near the dunes), the fuller the official program and the less the conferees leave the hotel; (3) There is no comparison so frivolous, so useless, so banal, that someone will not state it: two speakers analyze jazz as "democracy in action." Another sees a high point of community in the teamwork of the Boston Celtics.

During a drive along the water, he parodied the talks: went on for five minutes about the highway system being the true indicator of the relationship between the individual and the community. His parody contained the sentence, "When one studies history, one sees the past." Today he is astonished when the lecturer on "systems analysis," in all seriousness, speaks of highways in just that way.

C: List of rules about academic meetings to become longer. Necessary to make a start, as Williams says, "out of particulars."

D: The lecturer on systems analysis quotes (finally) John Stuart Mill: "A habit of analysis has a tendency to wear away the feelings."

E: Academic hyperventilation.

## 210862

He writes what no one may see: tape across the flaps of boxes
shuts up a mouth screaming with common desires better hidden.
So they say, while the smug bibliographer puts up shelving.

# MEMOIRS

# The Hours Musicians Keep

M Y   F R I E N D Roger called last night, and Dorothy, reading at
the kitchen table, gave me a look of bewilderment-going-to-alarm
when I held the phone to my ear but said nothing. I knew who it
was. I could hear a bass figure in ⁶⁄₈ time and knew that it was only
a matter of measures until a whistle would begin to the tune of that
hoary cornet solo, "The Carnival of Venice." If things went well,
the whistler might try the first variation from J. B. Arban's version
or Herbert L. Clarke's—the arrangement on which I soloed at the
New York State High School Music Festival in my senior year. But
there would be no attempt to whistle the cadenza at the start of Del
Staigers' fearful version: lip slurs so rapidly up and down that it was
rumored that Del Staigers, the redhead, could only play it drunk,
and it could be approached by only one high-school cornetist of my
acquaintance—my friend Roger.

In college, however, I would sit second chair to Artie Shaw (not
the clarinetist), whose father owned a dairy in Hornell and whose
credentials included, not only the ability to play Del Staigers' dia-
bolical cadenza, but also to hit double high C, a note my horn has
never known, on a cold cornet. He was the closest I would come to
the kind of range which was all the rage then and which reached
both its zenith and apex in the joint recordings of Maynard Ferguson
and Yma Sumac—he of the freak lip with a high range to rival Cat
Anderson's, she of the otherworldly Peruvian voice of five or more
octaves which could come up from the tombs or shriek like a bird.
Was her name really Amy Camus? There were existential rumors.

Music was my earliest way into the world of nighthawks, bohe-
mians (as we called them before the word "beatnik" arrived), and
culture. I played from the fourth grade on, eventually owning a hand-
made Bach cornet bought used from Ned Mahoney, who played

second chair to the Goldman Band cornet soloist, the always rapid, sometimes sloppy, one-armed virtuoso, James F. Burke, and an Olds trumpet model named for the legendary Rafael Mendez, who could play high C on a trumpet suspended by a string, and who had once destroyed his embouchure against a swinging door and had taught himself a new lip position for the mouthpiece. In Mexico to end a brief marriage which left me with a son, I would spend half a day searching out a beer garden where Mendez was appearing, only to learn that it was his day off. The trumpet named for him had first and third valve triggers with which to flatten notes otherwise sharp because of the normal characteristics of the trumpet, but I preferred to lip them down, and in fact I preferred the more flexible, warmer tone of the cornet to the colder penetration of the trumpet.

Most young cornet players with a normal embouchure used a Vega 2 mouthpiece, but Roger and I used a Bach 10½C. Its deeper cup produced a deeper tone, though there was a penalty when the player went high. Things could go wrong, and did. In the long run, trumpet players grew barrel-chested and fought their instruments all the way to heart attacks. In the short run, there were sore lips from long gigs (alleviated by the cushion-rim mouthpiece, which resembles an ordinary mouthpiece with a doughnut for a rim), sticky valves (we used trick fingerings to make up for a lack of valve oil, and Roger once soloed on "The Minnehaha Waltz" with a stuck third valve), and a convention that called for the drummers to fire blanks to punctuate the endings of marches—a loud addition said to have been popularized at the University of Michigan.

There were also plumber's helpers to wah-wah the white blues, plastic hand guards to save the silver or gold plating from a sweaty grip, clothespins to keep the music in sight during outdoor concerts, and sometimes a banana to increase salivation in the cottony mouth that afflicts the nervous soloist.

As a soloist, I was always nervous. At my high school graduation, I played Clarke's "Stars in a Velvety Sky," while my cap tassel swung in time. It's the trumpet music of Herbert L. Clarke which one hears, incidentally, behind the action in the movie "Hester Street," and it was a revelation to me, on first viewing the film, that someone else had noticed the melancholy at the heart of Clarke's lyrical solos for cornet.

Roger and I would drive to New York, two hours west, to take in a Goldman Band concert in Central Park and then go to Birdland or Basin Street or the Metropole. Burke would solo every night that the band played in Central or Prospect Parks, make a token move toward reclaiming his seat, and be summoned forth to play an encore, always something easier—"Dreams of Karen," for example, which was dedicated to Burke by its author, Roy H. Milligan, and which he would play at about one and a quarter times its normal pace. When he was on a run, one could hear the holes in the valves lining up with the openings of the slides with little explosions of spit and breath. Roger and I sometimes unfolded the score to that night's solo across our laps, and one night when Burke chose to ignore the high, optional counterpoint the soloist may play while the band carries the melody to a Goldman solo called "Scherzo," we looked up at him, and we thought he smiled down.

At G. Schirmer's famous music store, then at 3 East 43rd Street, we could appraise new solos from the Fischer, Fillmore, and Mills music houses, and we would ask to see more and more difficult scores before making a choice.

Going to Birdland to hear trombonists J. J. Johnson and Kai Winding, we were likely to see Miles Davis or Don Elliott, too. The stadium dates and big record-distribution routes had yet to weaken the club system for jazz, and the artists came to hear one another and sometimes to sit in. Even then, the beer came only in paper cups, to cut down on violence, and the drinks were hustled to tables little bigger than the napkins. Still, to teen-agers it *seemed* spacious and cheerful. We didn't know shit, but we knew something.

Elliott was interesting to us because he tripled on cornet, French horn, and vibraphone. The Modern Jazz Quartet and the Australian Jazz Quintet were new sounds, mixing jazz with the classical. Miles' solos were already ethereal, and he had begun to use a mute on all standards. Nobody knew Cannonball Adderley's little brother Nat yet, but I thought he was terrific. Thad Jones teamed up with bassist Charles Mingus, and, when Stan Kenton made what seemed to be a racist response to *Down Beat*'s jazz awards, Mingus published a long poem in reply. A Connecticut station played records by Shorty Rogers in what came to be known as the "cool" sound and, later, the "West Coast" sound when Rogers went off to work for Hollywood. The hottest trumpeter, to my mind, was Clifford Brown, whose records with drummer Max Roach were electric, and who would die young in an automobile accident. The trumpet had a value in those years it would never occupy again in a world of jazz that would never again seem so new, to anyone, nor evolve so rapidly, nor be so richly intertwined with an American lifestyle outside the mainstream.

And what does it mean that so many artists have come to their art by way of another art—writers, in particular, by way of music and painting? I believe I can distinguish between poets who came to poetry from painting and those who came to it by way of music: it goes beyond sound versus image, and is rooted in the difference between the populist spread of bands and group lessons in the public schools of small towns, and the parallel study of painting which, back then, was more likely to be undertaken seriously only by the urban and privileged. I'm afraid I still hear the difference when the band follows the orchestra, or vice versa, at the local junior high, though I hasten to add that I am talking now about childhood influences and not about professional accomplishment, and that there will never occur again, I believe, such clear lines in American culture. For one thing, we now see an increased participation in second-level artistic activity in our country which seems to derive from a feeling that everyone is important and no one is special. It is harder now, I think, to be an outsider unless one draws the lines on a political basis against most of America. It is possible, therefore, that what I, and others like me, took by way of lifestyle and attitude from the jazz world then must now come from the more greatly splintered sphere of racial, sexual, and revolutionary politics—in which it will prove increasingly difficult to align a literary majority to judge poets, or to give convincing approval to a handful of the "best." To me, these thoughts follow, as childhood trails middle age, waiting.

I knew I would never be good enough. I was insecure up high, I stayed too close to the chords on solos; worse, I saw notes when I played—the result of the way I had been taught, the only way I could have been taught. I quit the horn by not going to music school, though my trumpet teacher, Chester Osborne—a composer, historian, and author of serious books for youth—disagreed with my decision. I quit my musical future when I went to college, though I continued to play for several years: with a dixieland band on the radio, with orchestras, concert bands, marching bands, and dance bands. I played the "Trumpet Voluntary" by Jeremiah Clarke, long misattributed to Henry Purcell, on Easter Sunday in a black robe at the pulpit. I played duets with Lyle S. in fundamentalist churches in upstate New York. I jammed with friends in the college chapel. I even took lessons for two more years, and worked up additional solos by Haydn and Hindemith. Meanwhile, I taught myself to fake a popular piano. It was fun making it up, finding ways to make it come out well without being able to do it right.

Flutter-tongue and double-tongue. Pedal notes and shakes. *Schmaltz*, hand vibrato, and Montgomery Clift playing on just his mouthpiece in the movie version of *From Here to Eternity*. The half-valved neighing of a horse. Straight mutes and cup mutes. I played solos, duets, trios, quintets, sextets, with bands, orchestras, and combos. I played for fun and money but never to be better than someone else or even to have someone say so. Because of the hours musicians keep, I saw things differently, listened to different radio programs, and had time to think.

Six months ago, sitting in a Roman *piazza* on the outskirts of a fountain, I heard someone whistling "Carnival of Venice." I couldn't see who. If it was corny to identify so quickly, it would be far cornier to play the unaffected bystander. Was he whistling it well, or even correctly? It would not have occurred to me to care. And that's why poets are poets. And that's the name of that tune. And that's why Roger whistles me up twenty-five years later—old friend, Roger.

# What Became What: An Autobiography

C E N T E R  Moriches—a small, unsophisticated town—lies half-way out on the south shore of Long Island, sixty miles from Manhattan. I was born August 3, 1937, in a hospital in the Bronx, but I was a resident of Center Moriches from the start. My father, mother, older sister, and I first lived for several years on Chichester Avenue on what was considered the "wrong side of the tracks." Center Moriches held about two thousand people. The area was dotted by duck farms, truck farms, and potato fields. There were many roadside fruit and vegetable stands. There were many fishermen. The main thing was water: the Atlantic Ocean, the Great South Bay, Long Island Sound, Shinnecock Canal, inlets and creeks and ponds, coves and spits and sand bars, the docks and dunes, the beach grass, the tides. . . . A thin canal came all the way to Main in the center of town.

My best friend throughout grade school was probably Frankie Holzman, who lived across the street. His father, Frank, Sr., a house painter and the chief of our volunteer fire department, had been a fair first baseman, and he was keen to teach baseball to Frank, Jr., who wasn't all that interested. However, his older sister, Virginia, was, and often they played catch on the lawn in front of their house, with or without Frank, Jr. I'd stand around with my fielder's glove until Frank, Sr., would ask me to play, and then I'd stay as long as he'd let me, sometimes beyond his own children. I was like that: I couldn't get enough play, especially the kind of game in which you couldn't know for sure what would happen next: a ball over your head, a throw in the dirt—a chance for a great play!

What I know of my ancestry dates to the nineteenth century in the Ukraine. My father was the son of Marion Cardon and Mosha Botsian, both of Constantine, Russia. My mother is the daughter of Toba Suvrinsky of Taroscha, Russia, and Reuben Spector of Koshovator, Russia. I have my father's passport. He was a teenager when he immigrated to America, a tough-looking kid with short hair. First (and typically) his father and older brother, Harry, came to America. Once they had a purchase in the New World, the rest of the family followed. They had to leave at night, under a wagon load of hay, then ride bareback to Poland. Many other relatives came, also, generally settling in New York City or Boston. There was good reason to flee Russia, where both the czar's men and the Bolsheviks liked to kill Jews. My mother's parents had come to America earlier, as young adults. At the time, her future father was serving four years in the Russian army. Her future mother waited to marry him upon his discharge. But as his four years drew to a close, new fighting broke out, and the army refused to let him go. A generous man from my grandmother's hometown was financing the move to America, and it was time to go. So my mother's father and his fiancée simply met at the border, from where they escaped to London and then America.

My father did not speak Russian at home, and he rarely told stories of the Old Country. But those few he did, I remembered. I pictured my father slipping through trenches during the day to retrieve the bodies and hiding in the cellar at night while the czar's men and the Bolsheviks had it out. It was a lawless time. My father's family was poor, but his brother-in-law's was wealthy. One day, this man came home to find his family murdered. Afterward, he took revenge by walking the dangerous streets with his hands in the pockets of a fur coat—a sure sign of money and an invitation to trouble. Told to remove his coat by robbers, he would withdraw two pistols from his pockets and shoot them. It was a chaotic time, too, so that one could always hide in the woods. When the mayor's son bullied my father's sister, my father fought back and had to hide. When one of his brothers went to be examined for induction into the Russian army, and, asked at the end of the line if he had been accepted, lied and said no, the brother hid in the woods until the authorities stopped looking.

My father wanted his son and daughter to be Americans. And that is what I am: an American. I grew up on eastern Long Island, went to school in upstate New York, and later lived in both Syracuse and Rochester, but I no longer feel that I am primarily an East Coaster. I do not feel that I am a dyed-in-the-wool Midwesterner, either, even though I have lived in Chicago and Indianapolis, and have lived and taught in Iowa City since 1965. And I am not a full Northwesterner, though I have been hanging around the Northwest for a number of years and in 1985 purchased a small place in Port Townsend, Washington, where I have lived since, summer and winter, for part of each year. My sense of place comes from many regions of this country. Wherever we have been, I have worked for a living and we have gone exploring. Often we drive long distances: in the past year we have put thirty thousand miles on our car. Each year we drive from Iowa City to the far corner of the Northwest, and later back, sometimes by way of Canada. Often we have reason to follow that with a drive from Iowa City to mid-Vermont and back. And this year we drove from Iowa City to Santa Fe, then to Tennessee and down to New Orleans, and after that to Utah and on up to Port Townsend.

Truly, I feel connections to, and differences from, each place we have lived, and perhaps because there have been so many, each place is for me inextricably of the whole. I taught a trimester for Goddard College and lived in rural Vermont. I have lived and taught in Hawaii. I have lived in Santa Cruz, San Francisco, and Santa Fe. Outside the United States, I have lived in parts of Mexico and Spain, briefly visited Cuba, Guatemala, and Nicaragua, and traveled in eastern and western Europe, Morocco, and Australia. I feel that I am an American before I am of any one region—an American poet, with an American childhood, the changing American vision, American successes and failures, troubling American responsibilities. Can one be called a localist but not a regionalist? If so, then that is what I am. Had I traveled more in other countries, I would be pleased to be thought a citizen of the world.

But an autobiography must rest necessarily on one's childhood and early adulthood, for that is the time when emotion and instinct coalesce, and the vision planted then will flower, no matter what. And so, in December of 1990, I have returned to eastern Long Island for five weeks to write this report. This morning, walking the roads outside East Hampton near Sammis Beach (called "Sammy's Beach" by some cartographers), I passed a sign for "Hidden Drives." Grasping, some might say, at straws, even as I plucked a stem of beach grass to chew, I sensed a kind of code in that sign. It was signaling me, reminding me that our motives—our drives—remain hidden, as does the great wealth of cause-and-effect by which we arrive at a moment when we look back, autobiographically.

*Long Island*

The things I did, I did because of trees,
wildflowers and weeds, because of ocean and sand,
because the dunes move about under houses built on stilts,
and the wet fish slip between your hands back into the sea,
because during the War we heard strafing across the Bay
and after the War we found shell casings with our feet.
Because old tires ringed the boat docks,
and sandbags hung from the prows of speedboats,
and every road in every country ends at the water,
and because a child thinks each room in his house big,
and if the truth be admitted, his first art galleries
were the wallpaper in his bedroom and the carlights
warming the night air as he lay in bed counting.

The things I did, I counted in wattage and ohms,
in the twelve zones that go from pure black to pure white,
in the length of the trumpet and the curves of the cornet,
in the cup of the mouthpiece. In the compass and protractor,
in the perfect beveled ruler, in abstract geometry,
and if the truth be known, in the bowing of cattails
he first read his Heraclitus and in the stretching box turtle
he found his theory of relativity and the gist of knowledge.
He did what he did. The action of his knee in walking
was not different from the over-stretching of an ocean wave,
and the proofs of triangles, cones and parallelograms
were neither more nor less than the beauty of a fast horse
which runs through the numbers of the stopwatch and past the finish.

The things I counted, I counted beyond the finish,
beyond rolling tar roadways that squared the fields,
where I spun on the ice, wavered in fog, sped up or idled,
and, like Perry, like Marco Polo, a young man I saw
alone walk unlit paths, encircled by rushes
and angry dogs, to the indentations of his island.
And if the truth be told, he learned of Columbus,
of Einstein, of Michelangelo, on such low roads and local waters.
Weakfish hauled weakening from the waters at night,
and the crab rowing into the light, told him in their way
that the earth moved around the sun in the same way,
with the branched mud-print of a duck's foot to read,
and life in the upturned bellies of the fishkill in the creek.

I can't remember when I started to take walks, to go off alone,
talking to myself in my head, and, when I couldn't do that, to say
things on paper. Now my father had a small five-and-ten in a small

town. After getting his feet on the ground in America, he had left behind the cities where other Jewish escapees from the czar and the Bolsheviks congregated, striking out on his own, setting up shop against local advice in a building where businesses repeatedly had failed. And there he worked hard, happy to be his own boss, and prospered. By every standard that mattered to him he was a success: he supported his family, the community respected and liked him, and he was free. He had no objection to hard work of his own choosing, and he enjoyed the days, his customers and his family, no matter what. When I was born, he danced on the counter. He hid from his children the fact that he had heart trouble, and he died of a stroke just after I graduated from college.

But now I was walking out of our house on Union Avenue at all hours, especially at night, heading down to Main Street, away from the stores to the edge of town, then turning toward the Great South Bay on lampless streets, sometimes walking a route several times in succession. There were stops—to see what was in the camera store window, to take books from the small house that several nights a week served as the town library—but mainly I kept walking.

While I walked, ideas went through my head. I couldn't keep from thinking. Every little thing was a small, dry sponge, waiting for some bit of free flowing attention that would swell it to grand proportions. I had a habit of noticing *how* people said things. Nothing about my mind seemed odd or important to me, but it required of me time alone, the walking, and the darkness of night. Years later I would come upon Rilke's concept of an essential solitude, but I already knew that one could be alone in a crowd.

### How He Grew Up

He found the corner of town where the last street
bent, and outdoor lights went down a block
or so and no more. In the long list of states
and their products, there was bauxite, rope,
fire engines, shoes, even a prison, but not one
was famous for purposeless streets and late
walks. Often he missed the truth of lists
while gone for a walk, with most lights out
all over town, and no one told him, when he
returned, the ten things it was best to, or
the dozen it was better not to. He knew
the window would be lit most of the night

down at the camera shop, and the gentle
librarian would keep the house of books open
if he stopped by at closing. Up the street he went,
leaving the lamps, each night until he met
the smell of the bay, a fact to be borne home
to sleep, certain of another day. The houses of
friends were dark. He never told, in those days.
Something was missing from the lists of
best and how to and whose town did what.
He figured, when no other was mentioned,
it might be his town at the top of some list:
but it was hard to read things on paper
in the bony moonlight. So he never knew.
People ask him all the time to have been
where what happened happened, that made
the news, but usually the big things happened
while he was out walking: the War, the War, etc.

At the drugstore, I could buy *Writer's Digest* and *The Writer*. I
thought it must be wonderfully free to be a writer. By "writer," I as-
sumed journalist, columnist, or nonfiction free-lancer. I made lists of
subjects for articles. The columns of Sydney J. Harris, which some-
times showed a most undaily intellectual bent, appeared in one of our
newspapers, and I pictured a life in which one might live anywhere
and make a living by mailing back little daily essays.

In fourth grade, when the band instruments had been put on dis-
play, I had chosen the trumpet. In a small town with limited ideas
of expression, music was to be my first art. Chester Osborne, our
public school bandleader, himself an accomplished trumpet player,
was my teacher. He was also a composer, a writer of serious chil-
dren's books, and a historian. Later, as I approached graduation, he
would suggest that I attend music school, or, if I preferred—rarely
did anyone from Center Moriches or the nearby towns of Moriches,
East Moriches, Brookhaven, Mastic, Mastic Beach, etc., strike out
for college—join the Coast Guard band, but I chose not to. Although
I didn't know it, he was offering me a chance to find out about the
rest of the world. Years afterward, he would say that, while he had
feared at the time that I had thrown away my chances by giving up
music, because of my writing things had turned out okay after all.

One day in the middle of an English class, Mr. Berdan, our
teacher, suddenly said: "You know that stuff they tell you about
these being the best years of your lives? Well, don't you believe it.

It gets better and better." I liked him for that remark. I was already developing a sense that the conventional wisdom was often wrong.

I also liked Mr. Berdan for having once changed the requirements of a test in reply to my challenge that the requirements weren't fair. In fact, they were probably fair enough, but I never forgot the willingness of a teacher to listen, to change and to say, "I think I was wrong, and you are right." As a teacher, I have often said since, "You are right, and I am wrong."

I played in school bands, marching bands, summer bands, fire department bands, orchestras, duos, trios, quartets, quintets, sextets, combos. I often performed solo. In the New York State High School Music Competition, I played Herbert L. Clarke's version of "Carnival of Venice." At graduation, I played Clarke's "Stars in a Velvety Sky," which was used with other Clarke cornet solos in the sound track of "Hester Street": someone else had noticed the lilting melancholy in that part of each Clarke composition known as the "trio." I played with the Monday Night Band, an adult band which met on Tuesdays in Riverhead. These were good musicians under an admired conductor, Howard Hovey, and, to prove it, at each concert he had the band sight-read one composition. I didn't think about it, but the music was teaching me spontaneity. I was learning about freedom and individuality and beauty, and also the nature of an ensemble— from late nights and jazz. All the while, I kept walking. After I got a used car—it was a '50 Plymouth—I took rides, often ending up at the water just to sit and look out. When a hurricane was reported en route, I would drive through Westhampton Beach to reach Fire Island before the roads could be closed—to see the stormy Atlantic lapping the land.

My sister, Ruby, four years older, was to marry a man from East Moriches whose father was a "ham": an amateur radio operator. One Thanksgiving, Roy Raynor took me upstairs to his "shack," his radio room in the attic. I was transfixed. I sat for hours listening to shortwave stations. Later, I learned International Morse Code, took the appropriate Federal Communications Commission examination on electronics, and received a station license: W2IDK. I built a piezoelectric crystal-controlled oscillator and power supply that put out twenty watts. With it, I talked (in code) to radio operators in California and England, in the Canal Zone, and on Saint Pierre and Miquelon Islands. I specialized in handling "traffic" (messages routed by an elaborate circuit of "nets" of operators that meet at designated times and frequencies), and on certain days I served as "net control" for the Swing Shift Net, which convened on the airwaves during my school lunch hour. On those days, our homeroom teacher gave me a little leeway as she took attendance and I raced my bicycle up the school driveway. I had a fast and accurate "fist," and in code the others could not tell that I was not an adult. I liked that.

Amateur radio operators were odd ducks. I liked that, too. I pedaled my bike to nearby towns to meet them. Some took me under their wing. Roy Raynor, W2EBT ("Two Eggs, Bacon and Toast," he called himself, or "Elderly, Bald and Toothless"), was the first. Van Field, W2OQI, lived like a hermit, making radio equipment in a tiny house in the woods. He was a "builder," the kind of amateur radio operator who lives to make equipment from scratch and goes on the air only to test it. I spent many hours at his place, learning, and he helped me construct my first transmitter. It was necessary then to build one's first transmitter to earn credibility as a "ham." No kits allowed. One chose a schematic, bought the parts on Radio Row in New York City (Canal Street), cut the chassis to accommodate vacuum tube sockets, and went from there.

Another adult friend was Herbert Snell, W2FCH ("Two Females Chasing Herbie"). He gave me rides to and from the amateur radio club, and while we traveled he talked. He seemed to me an unconventional mind. All the amateur radio operators of those days seemed to me to have walked away. Upstairs in their "shacks," whether building, or handling traffic, or trying to work "DX" (distant stations, especially those in other countries), or experimenting with VHF and UHF, or just contacting other hams to chat, they were really escaping to a world in which they could talk to themselves.

I wrote a column about events at the school for the local weekly, and the sports editor let me hang around late at night. While he thrashed his way toward various deadlines, I prepared the baseball and basketball statistics.

There were ball clubs—I played on the soccer and basketball teams at school, and outside of school I played on Police Athletic League basketball and baseball teams. My father bought a small speedboat—an inboard—and sometimes I'd ride my bicycle to the inlet where it was docked and sit in it and daydream. We'd fish together, and for four years he picked me up after school three days a week to drive me to Patchogue, a bigger town than ours, located half an hour west, to study Hebrew and to prepare for my bar mitzvah at thirteen. We went to Friday night services in Patchogue, and I attended Sunday school there, with interludes of Friday nights and Sunday school in Riverhead, a town northeast of Center Moriches, depending on how my parents felt about the rabbis. Later, I attended Catholic masses with a Catholic friend, and over the years I have taken part in many different church meetings. Others may at times have identified me as Jewish, and certainly I was born to it, but I felt eclectic from the start. There were things about every philosophy and, thus, religion, that I liked, beginning with the social utility of churches and the power of belief. I enjoyed arguing with the rabbi, and I think he enjoyed it also. Later, I heard a lecturer at college say that, in Judaism, study was equivalent to prayer, and I thought to myself, "That's the part of me that's Jewish." My Judaism, as I saw it, was realistic, tough but fair, and it had a sense of humor. My father's standard response to criticism of someone else was to say, "Well, he has to make a living too."

### The Israeli Navy

The Israeli Navy,
sailing to the end of the world,
stocked with grain
and books black with God's verse,
turned back,
rather than sail on the Sabbath.
Six days, was the consensus,
was enough for anyone.

So the world, it was concluded,
was three days wide
in each direction,
allowing three days back.
And Saturdays were given over
to keeping close,
while Sundays the Navy,
all decked out in white
and many-colored skull caps,
would sail furiously,
trying to go off the deep end.

Yo-ho-ho, would say the sailors,
for six days.
While on the shore their women moaned.

> For years, their boats were slow,
> and all show.
> And they turned into families
> on the only land they knew.

And there were friends. We fished, played ball, rode our bicycles to adventures, and generally enjoyed the safe innocence of that time and place. What did we expect to be? Clerks, store owners, salesmen, mechanics, tradesmen, secretaries, maybe a coach or teacher or nurse. And of course volunteer firemen. Eastern Long Island then, as today, depended on well-trained and well-equipped volunteer fire departments, which competed in special tournaments each summer and formed basketball leagues in the winter. Few of us even considered college. During World War II, I helped watch for enemy airplanes at the official spotter station at the water end of Union Avenue.

Many of the students in our school came by bus, mainly from towns to the west. Few of us didn't leave Center Moriches when the school day ended. By high school, there seemed to be even fewer of us from town. Then a friend from Bellport invited me to a band concert at her high school. Bellport was a richer town, west of us and south of the highway, where families lived who had someone working at Brookhaven National Lab, formerly Camp Upton. She knew I was a hotshot cornet player, and she told me that their band had one, too, and that I should listen for the first-chair cornetist. The first chair was good, certainly, but the second chair, who played with an odd embouchure—the mouthpiece off-center, his head thrown back, his eyes looking down his nose—was terrific. His name was Roger Edwards, and we became lifelong friends. Summers, we played in the Bellport, Center Moriches, and Westhampton Beach bands. We formed a trumpet trio with Roland Smith—the "first chair" I had been told to listen for—and with others we formed a "combo" to play in bars. Roger and I sometimes drove to New York City to attend concerts in Central Park by the Edwin Franko Goldman band—James Burke was the trumpet soloist, and I had bought a Bach cornet from Ned Mahoney, Burke's second chair—after which we'd go to jazz clubs such as Birdland and the Metropole and to the live television of the Steve Allen "Tonight" Show. Roger and I could talk philosophy and laugh at the same time. Later, I learned that Kierkegaard had said that laughter is a kind of prayer. It certainly seemed so.

I came to know others in Bellport, especially Frank DiGangi, another lifetime friend. DiGangi sometimes played drums with us and, although we didn't yet know it, he too was headed circuitously for a life of creative expression. Recently, Frank's wife, Carole Worthington, who grew up in East Hampton when it was potato fields, and not a "second home" in sight, said that Frank, Roger, and I became friends because, "There was no one else." An exaggeration, perhaps, but not untrue.

*Music Lessons*

The best place to hear a cornet played is the local gymnasium:
the kind with a basketball court, a stage and a balcony
in which small public schools hold their songfests and dances.
The long waxy strips of the wooden floor are very like
the golden sounds of the B-flat cornet in bright daylight,
and the empty room in which so many bodies have passed
accepts and embraces each articulated musical phrase
with that warm sadness known best by the adolescent.

If I had never taken up the cornet, I sometimes think,
beauty would not have taken all my days and filled my thoughts.
If I had not had that free hour in the middle of the school day,
not selected a mouthpiece with a deep cup for its richer tone,
not carried it in my hand to warm it up ahead of time,
if I had never given in to the subtleties of an embouchure,
I would not have been blown about by every passing song,
each with its calendar and clock, each with its beloved.

It takes only a few measures for the dreams to get out,
and then you cannot stop them or make them go away.
A river of whole tones sweeps from the bell of the horn,
containing the sun and moon, the grass and the flowers,
all time, and the face of every kindness done to a boy,
and every object of his desire by name, and a single smile.
It was my good fortune to be the breath of a magic cornet
and my fate to fall asleep to music every night thereafter.

I applied to Alfred University because two people in town were graduates—a French teacher and a lawyer. I knew nothing about colleges, but my father thought I should go. I went off to Alfred wearing a leather jacket with a switchblade in one pocket. My parents had bought me a briefcase and the Hadassah had given me a suitcase. I assumed that Alfred was close to home—I had never been farther away than Boston and New York City, to visit relatives. Alfred turned out to be four hundred miles from Center Moriches, and I was late to orientation.

Alfred University is located in Alfred, New York, down the road from Alfred Station. Where is it, really? About sixty miles south of Rochester, in the southern tier of western New York. My freshman year it snowed September 14. We called it "Albert" and were amused by the school song, which referred to "Alfred, the Mother of Men."

At my interview for Alfred, which had taken place in a hotel room in New York City, the college representative warned me that in college I would have to choose among activities. I couldn't do it all. But I tried. I asked special permission each semester to take extra courses. I worked for the yearbook and the weekly newspaper, the *Fiat Lux*, and as a senior I edited the paper. I was elected to the student senate. I joined a fraternity, then resigned but stayed a "social" member. I hadn't quite given up cornet, and I took lessons from Dan Clayton, a music teacher who had returned to college to prepare for dentistry. I played with the university concert and marching bands and the town orchestra. On Easter, Dan Clayton and I put on black robes and played Purcell's "Trumpet Voluntary" from the pulpit. (Purcell gets the credit, but he didn't write it: Jeremiah Clarke wrote it.)

At Alfred, men were then required to take two years of Reserve Officers Training Corps. I went on to advanced R.O.T.C. At the time, it seemed wise—we all expected to be drafted out of college—and the pay for taking the advanced courses came in handy. Moreover, I was a Jew. I remembered Hitler. I had yet to meet a single conscientious objector. In 1957, I went through basic military training at Fort Bragg in North Carolina.

At Alfred, my eyes were opened by another group of "odd ducks." In the State College of Ceramics, located within private Alfred University, the design department had been subverted by artists. I had never known such people, mostly New Yorkers. They had a way of life—their work. It proved impossible to keep the ceramics building locked at night because they would break in to get back to work. During my late-night walks, I included in my route the bottom levels of the long ceramics building where I knew I would find, whatever the hour, printmakers, sculptors, and painters at work. These student artists didn't depend on what others thought. They had a "studio" mentality and so did their teachers—artists together, their lives centered in work and surrounded by good fellowship. To me, it was a revelation, and I watched them. They had talent, they were street smart, and they were actively in touch with their inner selves.

149

Slowly my eyes opened also to writers and writing—especially journalism. I took one creative-writing course. Dr. Finch required three short stories over the semester. I wrote them late at night in the student union, after it was closed. I knew the student who cleaned up. I'd come in the back door carrying a typewriter, we'd feed the jukebox and cook hamburgers, and then I'd write a story while he cleaned.

My friend and roommate, Lew Carson, wrote the best story of the class. I didn't know what Dr. Finch was getting at when he talked about an image in Lew's story. In it, the main character ended his day at an arcade, shooting a miniature bear behind glass—repeatedly hitting the glass eye on the bear's belly with the beam of light from his toy rifle, so that the bear groaned, stood up, and reversed its direction over and over. In the window of the machine, the shooter could also see his own face. Later, I understood the image, but not yet.

In *New World Writing*, I found an odd poem. It began, "Fuzz clings to the huddle." And its final line was, "We rise and leave with Please." I brought it to Dr. Finch who said he didn't know much about modern poetry and suggested I try Miss Tupper. Miss Tupper didn't know much about modern poetry either, but neither of them disapproved of my interest.

And I *was* interested. We all were. We had the rage to be artists. It was the fifties, a time of many constrictions which then seemed natural but now seem numbing. The part of America that we knew best was becalmed. The Beat Generation was coming, and we were its audience-in-waiting.

Roy Glassberg and Mike Moses wrote for the literary magazine. We ran around together and lived in the same rooming house. I knew that my composition teacher had published a novel, though he never mentioned it. One of the students—Charles Froome, one of many military veterans at the school—had published a book of poetry with a "vanity" press, but to me it was a book like any other. I was not part of the literary magazine scene but of the newspaper scene, where I began as a reporter and ended as editor in chief. Along the way, I also began a commotion.

It started with a review—mainly a summary—of a book about sectarian clauses in fraternities and sororities. My article brought a response from the vets on campus, who didn't think that a university should be housing groups that discriminated against minorities.

One thing led to another, and soon the campus was fiercely divided. By then I was managing editor to Nathan Lyons, a photographer, a vet, and a serious man who talked easily about both aesthetics and morality. I liked reading philosophy more than fiction. One of my heroes was the student who emptied his room, painted it white, and sat for days in a chair in the otherwise vacant room, thinking.

When there was cause, I wrote and mimeographed an "underground" newsletter, which then appeared on the auditorium seats on the Thursdays of college-wide assemblies. At first, few knew that it was I. Later, when people knew, the university tried to seal up the mimeograph machines in town. By then I had succeeded to the editorship and the crusade to get the university to take a position on sectarian clauses—one way or the other—had become even hotter. Newspapers in Buffalo and Rochester sent reporters to Alfred to cover the story. There were hairy encounters. I wanted the university to make a statement, but I was willing to accept any position they were willing to own up to, whether or not I liked it. However, I couldn't accept their silence, their refusal even to recognize that discrimination could be an issue. A local minister wrote me an encouraging letter and said that a good editor needs a hide of leather. He told me of a mimeograph machine in the church basement that I could use. But I didn't need it. I had a friend with a key to Hornell High School, where we were producing newsletters in secret in the middle of the night.

Dr. Sibley's ethics class was a favorite. When I asked if I could miss class to attend a talk by Ashley Montagu at the other college in town, the State College of Alfred, he agreed on condition that I report the event to the class. Montagu spoke on "The Natural Superiority of Women," based on chromosomes, and afterward, in a small informal group, he told an amazing story about two anthropologists from the University of Toronto, Edmund Carpenter and Marshall McLuhan. The story concerned their trip to the Aleutian Islands, and a way of seeing that enabled the Eskimos there to fix car and plane motors without having studied them. He told us how the first issue of *Explorations*, a Joycean magazine edited by Carpenter and McLuhan, came into being as a result.

Dr. Bernstein was a star among the students for his passion. He taught American literature. I took his special graduate course in literary criticism, meeting at night.

Summers, I worked as I always had, in my father's five-and-tens. He had slowly developed a clientele at a second store, in Mastic Beach: a town that filled up between Memorial Day and Labor Day with families from Brooklyn, Queens, and the Bronx. The summer of my junior year, I was scheduled to take army field training at Fort Bragg in North Carolina. The night before I had to go, typically I stayed up late. I had rediscovered an unused film-developing kit, and now I couldn't put it away without trying it.

Back at Alfred, I began to take photographs, developing and printing in the darkroom of the *Fiat Lux*. I still loved to stay up late. Looking back, I see that there are certain things about me that were true from adolescence on, and have not changed: I like to start work very late at night and then work until dawn, I like a workroom full of tables, and, when I can't sit still, I go for walks. Also, I talk to myself, silently, when alone. Always have. I should probably add to this table of constants the appeal that the arts have had for me, which is to say that I have wanted to try them myself—all of them. But I admit that I could probably be happy in nearly any honest job if my employer would allow me to work late at night in a room full of tables, with walk breaks and some silent extracurricular mental activity along the way.

John Wood was a master teacher among the design students, famous for his great silences and his enormous artistic productivity. He let me take a photography tutorial. First assignment: make a series. I did it—my series involved the horizon, and there were many tricks—and brought it to the design room to show him. It was R.O.T.C. day—once a week, we had to wear our uniforms—and I felt conspicuous among those students who were wilder and more artistic than I was. John Wood looked long at my series. He tried switching two prints and then put them back. He tried switching two others and returned them to their places. Then he said, "Good. Make another series." It was a fine tutorial.

As editor of the student weekly, I got caught up willingly in many issues. I believed journalism to be honorable work. So, after graduation, I enrolled in the graduate journalism school at Syracuse University. My old friend Roger was there completing a music degree, and I moved in with him.

Waiting to complete registration, I met another person who would become a lifelong friend, Al Sampson. He and I both had considerable newspaper experience—Al had graduated college ahead of his class and then gone off to be wire editor for the *Minot Daily News* in North Dakota. We discovered that we both had chosen journalism because of certain ideals and because—this was idealistic, too, and perhaps naive—we didn't want to ruin literature for ourselves by earnestly studying it for a graduate degree. But Syracuse didn't know what to do with us and made us take beginning copyediting courses and the like, which we soon skipped except for the exams. I liked Professor Root's course in "Social Responsibility and the Press," and I respected Professor Bird's "Research Methods," for which we had to write the equivalent of a term paper each and every week. On class day, Professor Bird would detail the exactitudes of the next assignment while bleary-eyed students straggled in, fell into their seats, and made one final proofreading of the paper due that hour. I enjoyed typesetting with Professor Norton in the Bodoni Labs.

Al and I, and Mary (Mickey) Mammosser—whom I met at an organizational meeting for the campus literary magazine, though neither of us returned—skipped other classes to read poetry in a restaurant near campus. I think it was called the Italian Villa. We read the Beats—Ginsberg, Corso, Ferlinghetti—and others to one another over afternoon salad and evening pizza. Al soon realized that the journalism courses were taking him nowhere and switched to English, but I decided to finish a semester before skipping out. Next Al decided that he would be better off studying literature at the University of Chicago in his hometown, and he left.

Mickey and I eloped and moved into an apartment on University Avenue. The super was a retired navy boilerman who liked to analyze the content of the Steve Allen Show and was rewriting the Bible. He had spent a summer reading the *Encyclopedia Britannica* on a beach. Handing over the monthly rent check to him was always interesting and took time. Meanwhile, the dean didn't approve of my having eloped with an undergraduate, and eventually he suggested I not return. I intended to leave in any case, and Mickey and I had already moved to Rochester, where we had taken an apartment on Evergreen Street. I interviewed for a job at Eastman Kodak. The interview took place in a small, almost bare room. It was a small, bare interview. I could feel the weight of the corporation as my interviewer told me about their training programs, the benefits, even the retired employees' sport center.

### The Delicate Bird Who Is Flying Up Our Asses

The delicate bird who flies up your asses
is flying up mine
also, with no express invitation.
The bird who likes the lean and hungry
is making me sweat.
I have delusions that I need a job,
that I will waste away
unless I eat the bird,
and that my family will remember me
only as a poor provider.
That bird means to straighten me out.
The bird in favor of fathers and sons
is cropping up insidiously.
Once I could be lazy;
now he turns up everywhere I sit.
Each day I have a feeling of the bird
higher within me.
Once I declined burdens;
now I jump to be responsible
for ones I haven't yet.
I can tell that bird
means to stay with me forever.
Hire me. I have another mouth to feed.

While in Rochester, Mickey and I began a magazine of literary and visual materials. We called it *statements*, without an initial capital. Nathan Lyons was now working for the Eastman House of Photography and he often employed the word "statement." To me, the word suggested clarity and thought with a philosophical tinge. I felt, even then, that the meaning in words was of more moment than any confusion in the use of words, and that poetry had important content.

Rochester was now a hot spot of creative photography. Minor White, who edited and published *Aperture*, taught at the Rochester Institute of Technology, and Walter Chappell and Nathan Lyons had introduced contemporary work into the Eastman House, while Nathan had thoroughly modernized its house journal, *Image*.

One night Nathan and I went to Minor White's home to attend one of his tutorials. He propped an abstract photograph on a music stand and we "read" it. The remarks had a psycho-spiritual slant, and I only listened. Walter Chappell was experimenting with "thoughtography," a term coined by George De La Warr, who had been working in England, from the premise that the mind gives off a kind of energy that can be recorded—in this case, on film.

Al had been sending us clippings, notes, matchbooks, menus. On them he wrote, "Come to Chicago!" And one night we decided to do it. We loaded the car, put out the garbage, left the rent for the super, and headed off to Chicago. (Within twenty minutes of our arrival at Al's apartment, our car had been burglarized.) There I enrolled in the university and found a job at the law library. We lived in Hyde Park, an area populated by radicals and artists. At first we lived above the Accent furniture store on the corner of Blackstone Avenue and Fifty-third Street. Later, we moved to a third-floor apartment in an old house on the corner of Fifty-second and Kenwood. At work I read law books.

More issues of *statements* appeared. Each issue had its own format—one time, we could afford a color cover. I was now writing poems and still photographing, but I had put aside my cornet and trumpet: I loved music more than I loved the cornet. These were exciting times in Hyde Park: there were continuous political arguments and periodic confrontations. Civil rights were at the forefront. One friend described himself as a "professional radical" and worked for the railroad. Others held office in this or that organization. I joined with them in argument and demonstration, but I held back from anything further. I was still my father's son, and I trusted neither the czar nor the Bolsheviks.

I was still in Chicago in 1959 when my father died suddenly of a stroke. The completeness of it, the finality of it, the look of his corpse, the unsaid, my future never to be known to him—I felt a bottomless emptiness inside, and I still do when I remember his burial. The town shut down in homage, I said prayers in Hebrew, and then I returned to Chicago.

### Ending with a Line from Lear

I will try to remember. It was light.
It was also dark, in the grave. I could feel
how dark it was, how black it would be
without my father. When he was gone.
But he was not gone, not yet. He was only
a corpse, and I could still touch him
that afternoon. Earlier the same afternoon.

This is the one thing that scares me:
losing my father. I don't want him to go.
I am a young man. I will never be older.
I am wearing a tie and a watch. The sky,
gray, hangs over everything. Today
the sky has no curve to it, and no end.
He is deep into his mission. He has business
to attend to. He wears a tie but no watch.
I will skip a lot of what happens next.
Then the moment comes. Everything, everything
has been said, and the wheels start to turn.
They roll, the straps unwind, and the coffin
begins to descend. Into the awful damp.
Into the black center of the earth. I
am being left behind. The center of my body
sinks down into the cold fire of the grave.
But still my feet stand on top of the dirt.
My father's grave. I will never again.
Never. Never. Never. Never. Never.

Mickey decided I should have a son and bore one in 1960. When, after a year and a half of marriage, we divorced, our son, Nathan, stayed with me. Later, I married my present wife, Dorothy Murphy, who bore our second son, Jason, in 1966. My story since 1960 is forever woven together with the stories of Dorothy, Nathan, and Jason, who have enriched my life by virtue of their great hearts, their uncommon good sense, their goodness, their laughter, and their wondrous minds.

### An Elm We Lost

On it we wrote a little essay
about who loved who.
Shade moves in the grass, never still,
and they still do.

I took the M.A. slowly, but eventually it was time to complete it. All that remained was the examination, but I would have to be enrolled. I chose a poetry writing course which met in the evenings at the downtown center of the university. The teacher was the poet John Logan.

Logan was a wonderful teacher for young poets. He read our poems aloud so beautifully that they took on the grace of our intentions despite the awkwardness of our steps. He so seriously discussed the content of our poems—looking at surfaces and underneath—that they took on the substance we had wished for them despite our limited experience.

At the end of the course, Logan invited me to be a member of the Poetry Seminar. It was not an academic course, but an informal group of Chicago poets which met with Logan once a month in the offices of Jordan Miller's newspaper-clipping service. Besides Jordan, at one time or another the group included Dennis Schmitz, Bill Knott, Naomi Lazard, Jim Murphy, Irene Keller, Barbara Harr, Jessie Katchmar, and others. Jessie liked to hold my poems of elastic free verse on their sides and claim that they resembled the skyline of Chicago. She had written a poem about a spider in her bathtub in which she said that the spider was writing on the tub in "spider Gothic."

Paul Carroll was part of the Logan circle. Paul had been the editor of the *Chicago Review* when the administration of the university banned an issue. The banned issue became the first issue of *Big Table*. It was an exciting time for poetry. Villiers, Ltd., printed many of the little magazines in England, and James Boyer May, their representative, edited a magazine called *Trace*, which was full of news of the "littles." Logan began a magazine called *Choice*, to which he had me contribute an article and a photo of the Chicago Water Tower.

It was an exciting time for photography, too. Both Aaron Siskind and Harry Callahan were teaching for the Institute of Design. Many of their students would become well known. I spent a lot of time at Rodney Galarneau's small storefront gallery and apartment on the south side near Comiskey Park. Another photographer friend was David Rowinski, who assisted Hugh Edwards, Curator of Photography at the Art Institute.

I had been stalling the army—I would have to go on active duty eventually—and now I wanted to delay it further. I felt that in Logan's Seminar I had stumbled onto the real thing—poets and poetry—and I wanted more of it right away. Logan told me of something even farther west than Chicago—the Writers' Workshop in Iowa City. I decided to apply to Iowa to study for a Ph.D. And I went off to Iowa City to be interviewed by Donald Justice. After a while, Don and I and Kim Merker—a printer and the founder of the Stone Wall Press—went bowling. I must have bowled well because—I was accepted.

Dorothy, Nathan, and I moved to Iowa City at the beginning of 1961 and stayed three years. For most of that time we lived in a tiny house with a big yard on Fifth Avenue in the cheap part of town. Our rent was seventy-five dollars a month. As usual, the front room served as my study, as our bedroom, and as the living room for company. I taught Rhetoric, the course in reading, writing, speaking, and listening required of freshmen. I taught the ordinary course, the advanced course, the remedial course. I turned down a fellowship in the Workshop to go on teaching Rhetoric, and I chose to remain in Rhetoric when my peers were thrashing about for promotions to literature classes. I early abandoned the Ph.D. program.

Donald Justice and Paul Engle taught the poetry workshop. Justice was a fine teacher, one of uncommon precision, good will, and decency. He could describe quality and defend our imperfections at the same time. There were many poets there during those years who would make their mark: Vern Rutsala, Mark Strand, Michael Harper, Lawson Inada, Mary Crow, Charles Wright, Dori Katz, George Keithley, Kenneth Rosen, Van K. Brock, and others. Al Lee was famous among us because he had already published in *Poetry*. Catherine B. Davis had appeared in an influential anthology, *The New Poets of England and America*. William Brady was the best critic among us. Some people seemed to have special standing. But I was busy teaching, writing, and photographing—and soon would be potting—as well as taking classes, and I had a family. In the midst of a swirl of literary fellowship, I still felt that I was following my own road.

The Writers' Workshop had a feeling about it similar to that of the Alfred design department, Logan's seminar, Hyde Park, and the photography department at the Institute of Design. It was a studio program. Writers came because they were writers. People did not come to be made into writers, but to have the luxury of living among other artists as they themselves tested their commitment and their direction. The emphasis was on the writing and the social play that surrounded it. We discussed almost everything about poetry, but there was little talk of magazines or publishers or literary standing. Because Iowa did not then permit the serving of liquor by the drink, and beer was limited to 3.2 percent alcoholic content, the bars closed at 10:00 P.M. weeknights and 11:00 P.M. weekends. Artists and writers crowded together nightly at Kenney's. At closing, there would be a party: if no one had volunteered, the word would simply start from some corner of the room that the party tonight was to be at so-and-so's, and then nothing could prevent it. A few of us also favored Donnelly's, where artists from all over mixed with towns-people. Friday afternoons I joined a group in Donnelly's known as the "seminar"—the name reminded me of Logan's group. I was the group's only poet. We were older students, all apprentices in the Rhetoric Department, all given to laughter, philosophizing, and a certain edge of realism.

The fifth and final issue of *statements* appeared from Iowa City— a double issue of *statements* and *Midwest*, R. R. Cuscaden's maga-zine from Chicago. It was a collection of *Iowa Workshop Poets 1963* and contained a single poem by each of twenty-five poets.

On warm weekends the writers played softball. One day while I was fielding ground balls at third base, in between innings, the shortstop—the poet Keithley—told me of the Bay of Pigs invasion of Cuba then in progress. He knew before the rest of us—he had heard it from a relative by phone—and I was amazed.

John Schulze, a professor of design, started a photography course in the art department. There were many sets of fresh eyes in that group, and we created photographic exercises that were used for years afterward. I took a film course and, with a partner, made a short movie which began with a highly symbolic egg rocking in a cage and included a woman misapplying her lipstick and Bill Brady in his underwear lifting weights. Years later, I was told that film makers from the Polish Academy had come to town and praised it, but I have not seen it since.

Meanwhile, Henry Holmes Smith had decided to organize the creative photographers and called for a meeting at the University of Indiana, where he taught. Paul Engle gave me funds from the Work-shop to attend. Dorothy, Nathan, Nathan Lyons, and I shared a storefront apartment in Bloomington. Aaron Siskind came, and Art Sinsabaugh, and Jerry Uelsmann, who was then Smith's student, and Ansel Adams, and many others. We showed our pictures, looked at Maya Deren films projected onto a large wall two at a time, and posed for Sinsabaugh's huge portrait camera, which he had masked to make long horizontal pictures of the Midwest.

I had begun to throw pots. My teacher, Carl Fracassini, was the closest I was to come to a teacher in the spirit of the Zen masters.

He could teach without teaching. The pot shop—like the Writers' Workshop, housed in wooden World War II "temporary" barracks—buzzed with activity. The potters made clay in large plastic garbage cans, and, in other garbage cans, many of them also made beer. An apothecary in town stocked hops.

"Frac," as he was called, also taught a course simply called "Studio," required of beginning art majors and devoted largely to drawing. I was famous for my inability to write by hand legibly, and I had mentioned that I couldn't draw. Frac insisted he could teach me, and I enrolled in his studio class. By the end of the semester, I better understood drawing, and I had improved, but, no, I couldn't draw. I know now that one can do anything if one keeps at it and does it in whatever way one has to, but I didn't know it then.

One day Frac took me to Vance Bourjaily's farm to shoot clay traps. I could shoot a rifle with some accuracy, but I was missing with the shotgun. Then Frac swung his gun across the sky in demonstration: "Don't aim," he said, "point." Within a few minutes, I was picking off three clay pigeons at a time. That's the kind of teacher Frac was.

One summer when I was throwing only bottle shapes, Frank DiGangi and his wife, Carole—also an Alfred graduate, a potter and painter—came to visit. School was out, but I had the key to the pot shop. By now, Frank had left engineering—he had arrived at Alfred a year after I did, to attend the ceramics college—and had turned to sculpture. I knew that Alfred required an intense summer potting workshop of its design students. So off we went to throw some pots. And when I looked over at him, this man who was not a potter, I saw someone throwing effortlessly. Clearly, this was the way it was supposed to be. I, on the other hand, struggled to make my pots. Indeed, by throwing only bottle shapes, I was (symbolically?) closing down the opening at the top of each vessel. The next day I broke my bisqued pots and turned in the key, and I have not thrown a pot since. But today, three decades later, Hampton Potters, a pottery on the east end of Long Island operated by Frank DiGangi and Carole Worthington, produces extraordinary ware. The DiGangis estimate that in the past fifteen years they have produced about forty-five thousand pots. They have perfected glazes amazing for their vibrancy of color. And they underprice their pots, in my opinion. They still manifest the studio mentality I first saw at Alfred and which existed for me later in Chicago and then Iowa City.

*Drawn by Stones, by Earth,*
*by Things That Have Been in the Fire*

I can tell you about this because I have held in my hand
the little potter's sponge called an "elephant ear."
Naturally, it's only a tiny version of an ear,
but it's the thing you want to pick up out of the toolbox
when you wander into the deserted ceramics shop
down the street from the cave where the fortune-teller works.
Drawn by stones, by earth, by things that have been in the fire.

The elephant ear listens to the side of the vase
as it is pulled upwards from a dome of muddy clay.
The ear listens to the outside wall of the pot
and the hand listens to the inside wall of the pot,
and between them a city rises out of dirt and water.
Inside this city live the remains of animals,
animals who prepared for two hundred years to be clay.

Rodents make clay, and men wearing spectacles make clay,
though the papers they were signing go up in flames
and nothing more is known of these long documents
except by those angels who divine in our ashes.
Kings and queens of the jungle make clay
and royalty and politicians make clay although
their innocence stays with their clothes until unraveled.

There is a lost soldier in every ceramic bowl.
The face on the dinner plate breaks when the dish does
and lies for centuries unassembled in the soil.
These things that have the right substance to begin with,
put into the fire at temperatures that melt glass,
keep their fingerprints forever, it is said,
like inky sponges that walk away in the deep water.

Before leaving Iowa City, I would stop photographing, too. But first I stopped using film. I took the camera out, set it up on a tripod, adjusted the swings and tilts and bellows and lens, and looked, but I took no pictures. In the darkroom, I used the enlarger to create multiple images by printing through pieces of newspaper: pictures and text. Eventually, I no longer used either the camera or the dark-room. I had abandoned the cornet because for me it was the wrong instrument. I had stopped potting because I myself was the wrong instrument. But when I turned from photography I did it because I felt that I had learned what I could from it. Others might learn more, but I was finished and, if I continued to photograph, could only hope to document what I already knew. I believed that if I ever were to feel the same about writing poetry, I could walk away from it, too.

But then it was time to go on active duty. On New Year's Eve of 1964, while the sounds of our friends partying came to us from around the corner, Dorothy and I loaded the largest U-Haul we could rent. At midnight, we dug two bottles of beer from the snow and said a toast. Things were already looking up: just two weeks earlier I had received a transfer from the infantry to the adjutant general's corps.

I reported to Fort Benjamin Harrison, outside Indianapolis. During my training, we lived in a town appropriately called Fortville. I commuted to the post with a sergeant who was about to receive a direct commission to second lieutenant. I had postponed going on active duty so long that I had been promoted to first lieutenant. Our training class had many "noncoms" in it. My commuting partner noted that, as a sergeant, he kept two reminders taped to the rear of his desk nameplate: (1) "Keep the Old Man informed"; and (2) "Don't sweat the small stuff." I felt reassured by his advice. (Later I learned the corollary to #2: "It's *all* small stuff.")

I had been assigned to go next to the Army Information School, then at Fort Slocum on David's Island off Manhattan. But one night, during a class party, a major told me to report to him the next morning and, when I did, he asked me to stay at the Adjutant General School after graduation to become Foreign Military Training Officer. It would be an interesting job—running a liberal arts program for men and women from other countries who had come to take military courses. It would require irregular and sometimes long hours, and the job demanded initiative, so the major was asking me, not ordering me, to take the position. All I knew about my upcoming job at the Information School was that I was to be an assistant to the Director of Instruction.

I said yes. In deciding to favor the job over the location, I made the first of what were to be repeated decisions not to go back east. To my literary friends, it would appear strange to turn down a chance to be near Manhattan, and I wondered if I were making the best decision. Then again, because the major had handpicked me for the job, I had some bargaining power, and I used it to win authority to live off-post. We moved into one side of a duplex on College Street in Indianapolis.

I had a language lab, and authority to take my foreign soldiers on tours of factories, galleries, and museums. For the first half year or so, in addition to being Foreign Military Training Officer, I had other jobs. I was Public Information Officer, Assistant School Secretary, and Assistant Security Officer, and I served briefly as Company Commander.

As Foreign Military Training Officer, I set up a weekly series in which foreign soldiers could talk about their countries to the American soldiers. Inevitably, the people from other countries spoke of their countries' art and culture. When it was Major Yoshikatsu Yatsunami's turn, he appeared in a Kabuki costume, and began by leaping from the stage to taunt Colonel Sadove.

In Indianapolis, we met Sue and Terry Friedman. Sue was editor of *Signet*, a little magazine. The Friedmans had adopted children with problems, most recently Jamie, a hemophiliac. As I got to know the Friedmans, I discovered that the Indianapolis Hemophilia Association was so in debt to the local blood banks that they were in danger of being cut off. Yet repeated transfusions were exactly what a hemophiliac needed to prevent the otherwise crippling effects of bumps and falls.

The post was committed to its own Red Cross blood drives. But there were always hundreds of "casuals" around who were in between assignments and thus not attached to any local unit. Sergeant Theall was my Information counterpart in the Finance School, also located at Fort Harrison. He and I would line up the casuals and ask for volunteers. On the appointed day, the hospitals in Indianapolis would be ready with extra nurses. Army buses would bring in the donors, Henry's Hamburgers would donate juice and burgers afterward, and the post photographer would take pictures for the papers. We easily wiped out the debt. And when Sergeant Theall retired, he got the Army Commendation Medal he had always wanted, and deserved.

Dorothy and I made excursions from Indianapolis in three directions: to Ball State in Muncie, to Purdue University in West Lafayette, and, especially, to the University of Indiana in Bloomington. One summer, the School of Letters brought in John Logan, Nathan Scott, and Henry Rago, the editor of *Poetry*. I had been coming down to sit in on gatherings of poets—Clayton Eshleman, Mary Ellen Solt, Daphne Marlatt, and others—and this group was invited to give a reading during the big week. I was nervous about this because I knew it might mean meeting Rago, who had published me in *Poetry*. It did mean meeting Rago. He was considerate and learned, and I trusted him. I came to see how carefully he edited *Poetry*, then a touchstone among poetry magazines. Whether he accepted or rejected one's poems, I discovered, he paid attention and kept track and waited. After I came to know his ways, I made a practice of sending all my poems to him once a year in a big package. I maintained this practice until his death.

As my time in the army came to a close, I was asked to return to the Writers' Workshop to teach. The news came during the aforementioned session of the Indiana School of Letters, and one night in a restaurant I told Logan, my old teacher. He was delighted, but one of the Bloomington poets who was there was not. I learned from his response that writers who knew nothing about Iowa City or the Workshop nonetheless had many assumptions about it. Over the years, I would encounter this prejudice many times, and it would sometimes affect the reception by others of my poems. As the American poetry scene became more splintered, and the prizes multiplied, I noticed a certain cowardice among my contemporaries. Certain compatriots from my student days, and, later, students from my teaching days, kept their time at the Workshop secret when they broke into print, or they lied about it. I came to see that the success of the Workshop had made it a target. But I also came to see that it was an inevitable part of the literary life to be a target—outside the studio, writers could be envious and paranoid—and, in any case, from experience I already knew the Workshop to be honorable, exciting, and worthy.

But now I was being discharged from the army and we were off to Iowa City again, a town I had liked on first setting eyes on it. A letter from Engle helped me to get a three-month "early out" for "seasonal employment." As a member of the National Council on the Arts, Engle had been dining at the White House with President Johnson, Secretary of Defense McNamara, and Attorney General Robert Kennedy, and his letter made note of it. The Vietnam War was heating up faster and faster, and there was a rumor that junior officers like myself would soon be frozen for the duration. I was advised to have the documents signed quickly.

I went off to Chicago to obtain one final signature at Fifth Army Headquarters. I stayed with Aaron Siskind, who knew me as a poet and photographer and was amused to see me in the morning in my uniform.

I owed the army two weeks beyond the start of the first semester in Iowa City. We found a house on Iowa Avenue, I greeted my students on the first day of classes, and Dorothy and Nathan stayed while I went back to the post to live in the bachelor officers' quarters for my final two weeks in the army. The day I was discharged, I drove off the post singing out the car window.

The Vietnam War was growing fast. As Foreign Military Training Officer, my work had involved me with embassies, the State Department, and the Continental Army Command, as well as with visiting generals from our country and abroad. Because I often had to get things done quickly, I knew the noncoms—who run things. And so I knew that the military did not want the war. I had been reading dispatches that argued that we didn't belong in Vietnam and couldn't win in any case. Thereafter, I took part in activities protesting the war, but I could not blame just the soldiers. I blamed the government. I blamed all of us.

> *A Primer about the Flag*
>
> Or certain ones. There are Bed & Breakfast flags.
> They fly over vacancies, but seldom
> above full houses. Shipboard, the bridge can say
> an alphabet of flags. There are State flags
> and State Fair flags, there are beautiful flags
> and enemy flags. Enemy flags are not supposed
> to be beautiful, or long-lasting. There are flags
> on the moon, flags in cemeteries, costume flags.
> There are little flags that come from the barrel
> of a gun and say, "Bang." If you want to have
> a parade, you usually have to have a flag
> for people to line up behind. Few would
> line up behind a small tree, for example,
> if you carried it at your waist just like a flag
> but didn't first tell people what it stood for.

In Iowa City, I taught with Donald Justice and George Starbuck. Paul Engle was still part of the Workshop but was gradually moving out of it to establish the International Writing Program. There would be many, many colleagues over the years and a stream of talented, interesting, sometimes brilliant students. Donald Justice and I worked together for many years before he left to complete his academic career in his home state at the University of Florida. Robert Dana had restarted the *North American Review*, and for five years (1965–69) I served him as poetry editor. Later, I served as poetry editor for the first two years of the *Iowa Review* (1969–71) under its founding editor, Merle Brown.

Looking back at the years in Iowa City since I returned to teach in the autumn of 1965, I see signals about myself embedded in the decision to return and in decisions since to stay. Iowa City is one of the last of the big-college small-town towns. I am a small-town person. I like to greet people as I walk through town. I like a place where the weather gets "bad" by other people's standards. I like a place where people are less sure of themselves than they are in sophisticated cities. Iowans are truly friendly and believe in schools. Iowa is not at all what some of my friends on the east and west coasts think about it, but I have noticed that people tend to think their own place best and other places inferior. Iowa City is a secret many people know. It's been a good place for us, Iowa City—I'll let it go at that.

Teaching in the Writers' Workshop and elsewhere, reading at venues around the country and sometimes abroad—such activities have put me in the presence of hundreds of known writers. I have seen great modesty and irritating careerism. And I continue to harbor my affection for the studio sense of things—the Alfred design, the Institute of Design model (Moholy–Nagy, the Bauhaus), the old Writers' Workshop example. To me, the excitement is all in the writing and in a community of writers. As a teacher, I have tried to be a student. I take the position of a writer, not an expert. I have tried to remain in certain ways a beginner. My seminars have often included writing assignments, often simply a charge to "be influenced" by a book the members of the class have been reading together. In such cases, I have two rules: (1) No one has to write a "good" poem; and (2) teacher has to do the assignment too.

In the mid-seventies, the editors of *The American Poetry Review* asked me to contribute a regular column. I called it "Homage to the Runner," by which I meant to signal the long haul and some of the essential solitude from which writing is born. Following my bent, I wrote spontaneously and informally, following my nose while hoping to be useful. Like the teacher who does his own assignments, myself as an example. In other words: no smoke, no mirrors, no lords and ladies. I included poems in the articles. I hoped to demystify what did not need to be mysterious and to protect the unknown. Some of those essays later appeared in a prose book, *Old Snow Just Melting*.

There came a time when I began to run on the roads. I ran marathons and shorter routes and collected drawersful of race shirts. My column title had not meant that. But by the time the editors of *The American Poetry Review* convinced me to write the column again, I had given up running for more walking, and so I was able again to call it, "Homage to the Runner."

In 1990, I began again to write these regular essays about the processes of writing and reading. I thought about how things had changed and not changed. I counted up the things I still thought about writing. I looked at the ways in which I had changed, and I wondered how much was due to my writing, and before that to my walks and to my thoughts alone. I knew that the question was chicken-and-egg and could not be answered. But when I returned recently to Center Moriches High School, to speak about writing, I saw myself and my prospects in the classrooms, and I knew that something had made a difference. And so I tried to recommend, however lightly, my own dumb luck—born of other places and other people.

Down the years of Iowa City as home base, teaching and writing have given our family opportunities to live elsewhere for short periods. When in 1967 the University of Iowa gave me money just to write over a summer—a bonanza!—we drove to Marfil, a small town in central Mexico up the mountain from Guanajuato, and later to Ajijic. In the seventies, while teaching at Goddard College (it was then one of the most radical colleges in the country), we lived on a road with no name outside Moretown, Vermont. Later on, I worked a semester for the University of Hawaii, following it with half a year in Seattle, where I taught a bit for the University of Washington. In Spain we lived in Nerja and Sitges during a sabbatical. Work and occasional fellowships have taken us also to Australia, Morocco, and western Europe. Alone, I have gone to Italy and Yugoslavia and returned to Tangier and Marrakesh. We have spent sabbaticals in Santa Fe and in California—Santa Cruz and San Francisco. In recent years, Dorothy has often accompanied me on reading circuits and to writers' conferences.

*Acceptance Speech*

My friends,
I am amazed

to be Professor
in a University

seven times larger
than my home town

and all because
I went away. Meanwhile,

the roots of the ivy
just went on crawling

in the dirt in the dark,
the light that was Brady's

and Gardner's during
our Civil War

became the blaze
in Southeast Asia

and soon everywhere
men lay down

without their women
which is what can happen

when people like me
leave home hoping

to be promoted
and end up promoted

to the rank of Captain
and discharged honorably

just before
whatever new war

we should always have known
was always coming

out of torn pockets and salt
from needles and patches of flowers

out of places for lost birds
night fog and a dying moon

from the work we do yea
(death being

what we don't do).
So to be at work

offending death
which others welcomed

who left home too
and no differently

seems to me half
of a famous story

I have never read
even in school.

At the time that the invitation to return to Iowa City arrived, I had my sights set on a job anywhere in the Northwest. I had not seen the Northwest, but it called to me. Twenty years passed, during which our second son, Jason, was born in Iowa City in 1966, and we moved from the house we had rented on Iowa Avenue into a house of our own on East College Street. Then, in 1985, we purchased a small house in Port Townsend, Washington, at the same time that I was able to stop teaching summer school. Now we live in it between school years. Otherwise, others live there. I call Port Townsend "the Long Island of the Northwest," just as, here on eastern Long Island, I call Long Island "the Quimper Peninsula of the East." Our friends in Port Townsend say about us that we "live in Port Townsend and winter in Iowa."

I come from a long line of people who had to make a living. As for my books: yes, my inner being and some of my outer life are represented or expressed in them. But my books are the tip of the iceberg: underneath the surface, out of sight, lie hundreds of poems unfinished, poems finished but unpublished or published but uncollected, lectures delivered but never printed, notes for essays, pages from journals, unsent letters. . . . *The Escape into You*, a sequence of poems published in 1971, contains but half of the poems I wrote in that mode. The baker's dozen to and about my father—a series titled "You Would Know," which appears in the collection *Residue of Song*—are only part of a book's worth of such poems. Many poems from earlier books did not make it into the *New and Selected*. And there are those poems expressly commissioned to be printed elsewhere: long poems about the photography of Robert Heinecken and the paintings of Georgia O'Keeffe, and a piece for the inaugu-

ration of University of Iowa President James O. Freedman in 1982.
I titled this last-named, "On Second Thought, I Think We Should
Keep These Colleges Going." With guitarist Mark Daterman, I have
made a poetry-and-jazz audio tape. Frank DiGangi and I have dis-
cussed combining poetry and clay. When in 1990 it came time to
publish *Iris of Creation*, I found myself with three books' worth of
recent poems. I am one of those who is helpless not to write and
helpless not to change.

Yet if all my writing were collected and its content apprehended—
of nature, love, and politics; the stances, viewpoints, and vision; the
outer textures, the inner corridors of ideas, the verbal maneuvers—
still more would remain beneath the surface, out of view. For me—a
small-town person trusting dumb luck as much as thought, helplessly
receptive to the unconventional and the intimate—writing comes out
of a life. In such a rich and difficult world, I feel myself to be of
many minds at the same time and to have lived several lives at once.
Doesn't everyone?

# Entry for *The Poets' Encyclopedia*

FIVE-AND-TEN

*Five-and-Ten*: A kind of American store, found now only in small towns considered "backward." Real Five-and-Tens have wooden floors and fixtures, carry a little of everything common but nothing rare or expensive, do not sell medicine or groceries, do not advertise or cut prices, and were largely run out of business by the loss-leaders of large American corporations with the blessing of the American government, which has a parasitic relationship to large business. The Five-and-Ten made its money selling thread, socks, and drinking glasses. The register was always at the front, and the word *stealing* had not yet been changed to the word *shrinkage*. The store's profits rested on inventory and goodwill. If a store's shelves revealed empty spaces where small items had not been replaced when sold, you could be certain that the store would fail. The name of a failed Five-and-Ten was soon torn down to give a better businessman a chance, but the name of a good store was money-in-the-bank, and a new owner would have to pay extra for the "goodwill." A man's father, after several heart attacks, sold his Five-and-Ten and retired, but he couldn't stand it because in those days the Five-and-Ten meant service and the friendship of one's customers as well as personal success. It couldn't have happened in Russia, so the immigrant Five-and-Ten owners often came out of retirement to die in their stores. One owner knew no songs but sang all the time. A dog who was run over by an automobile got well in the back room. The Five-and-Ten, for those who knew it, is like a coloring book on a rainy day, when toy sales boomed. Because the Five-and-Ten sold little things—thimbles, rulers, birthday candles—the distinctions between things still seem important (one might say, primary) to one who grew up handling them. It is possible, therefore, for such a one to believe that language begins in the (mathematical) concept of unity and separation, and that poetry is a way of using meaning (for which the ordinary dictionary is the final arbiter) to apprehend Meaning (for which experience is the source and this kind of Dictionary/Encyclopedia the testimony) and make it known. Notions, "fancy goods," and trinkets. Less is more. Everyone knows what a thimble is. The General Store was friendly. The Five-and-Ten was *personal*.

# ESSAYS

# The "Technique" of Rereading

G O D knows, there exist more techniques for writing than are usually acknowledged. Probably, each of us uses a hundred or more all at the same time. Some of them may occur before a word is put to paper. For example, you go for a walk because you have noticed that afterward you feel like writing. Or you stay up extra late because you have noticed that after midnight you somehow elude the more banal levels of rationality. Or you begin to get up earlier than the rest of the family because you have noticed that, by afternoon, the poetry you might have written has gone into caring for the children. Or you sharpen twelve pencils because a better first line seems to emerge after a little stalling. Or you use a fountain pen, or a typewriter, or examination bluebooks, or yellow paper, or lined pads, or a quill pen. You smoke or drink coffee. You don't smoke or drink coffee. Like Hart Crane, you drink cheap wine and play Ravel's "Bolero" on the phonograph. You walk about. You pull your hair. You eat your beard. You sit in the corner of the cafeteria during lunch hour. You sit at the kitchen table after breakfast. You hide in a studio out back where you scheme to build a trapdoor and a tunnel to the sewers of Paris. These are "Writing Techniques." If you are lucky and talented, you may not need much else. You will be able to do your best work by adapting the method suggested for painters by W. M. Pirsig in *Zen and the Art of Motorcycle Maintenance*: "Make yourself perfect and then paint naturally."

Certainly, that seems a worthy goal: gradually to replace labor with inspiration, to achieve in maturity that condition in which poetry arrives as easily, as Keats would have it, as leaves to trees.

*In the meantime*, which is where we generally find ourselves, we need among our stores of writing techniques a method for noticing the little things in language, and for seeing how others did, consciously or unconsciously, all that we hope to do later by nature.

That method is rereading. Not reading but *re*reading. We all know readers who have looked their way through great libraries of books without absorbing any. On first reading, such readers may experience a poem as fully as any of us, but their experience of the poem is perforce limited to the least experience of reading and to the associations a text may stir as one's thoughts wander.

Reading as a writer is another matter. Language is a reflexive medium, even for the most unconscious of poets. In addition, writing usually assumes a strong linear base—one word at a time. Self-reflexive and linear, a poem read once has not been fully read. To learn from language itself and from poetry, we think about *how* it says what it says, as well as *what* it says. You must know and, knowing, you must be able to say. If you cannot say it, you probably don't know it.

There is another side to this. Learning to reread your own work and others' is vital to those of you who intend to go on writing because you must learn how to continue to educate yourselves in the absence of teachers. Everyone knows that writers' conference conferee in search of answers that would at once kick his or her writing up a level. In applications to the program for which I teach, we sometimes note that an applicant has studied with A through M in school, and also N through Z for periods of a week or two during summers. Teaching *can* make a difference, but only for the self-reliant.

Sometimes a student brings me poems that have already been discussed by another teacher. In such cases, the poet must be taking votes, right? "The other guy said this poem was bad but you like it, so it must be a good poem after all." Or, "The other guy liked it, so what does it matter if you don't? I was just checking your taste."

I get questions about writing that are based on there being a "correct" way to say a thing, or to lineate a free verse poem, or to begin or conclude or. . . . But you know the questions. Not one of them has an answer. The plain truth is that, except for mistakes that can be checked in the dictionary, almost nothing is right or wrong. Writing poems out of the desire to find a way to be right, not wrong, is the garden path to dullness.

You have to learn to learn, if you're serious about writing. It's not that hard. First, you should realize that no teacher is going to tell you all that he or she knows. Second, however much he or she tells, you will hear only as much of what is said as you are able to at the moment. You can take from a given teacher a few tricks, perhaps one or two ways of writing, but what you might better seek beyond that, for the long haul, is an attitude toward writing and an attitude toward how to read as a writer.

Reading as a writer is not the same as reading as a nonwriter. The writer is looking for what he or she can use. The writer reads on the edge of his or her chair. The writer goes slowly and doubles back.

Teachers were my teachers when I went to school, but poems have been my teachers since. I don't say *books*, but poems—one by one. Reading, or perhaps just scanning, entire books of poems is what the critic does when he or she discusses style or theme. In an ideal world, I sometimes think, we would not review books at all—as if individual poems did not have content. We would write reviews of single poems. Come to think of it, students often do that. Is it possible that it's students who are on the right track?

Nor need you wait to be "tempted," like they say, to reread poems. Poems are not movies; one doesn't lie back in the dark and demand stimulation. You go forward. At least, you lean a little. In part, that's what poetry is: a quality you experience because you pay special attention to the language.

Richard Wilbur's poem "The Writer" is an accomplishment of sanity and intelligence. It is also a fine example of how one small move in the language can lead to others, and how poetic showmanship can lead to serious concern.

*The Writer*

In her room at the prow of the house
Where light breaks, and the windows are tossed with linden,
My daughter is writing a story.

I pause in the stairwell, hearing
From her shut door a commotion of typewriter-keys
Like a chain hauled over a gunwale.

Young as she is, the stuff
Of her life is a great cargo, and some of it heavy:
I wish her a lucky passage.

But now it is she who pauses,
As if to reject my thought and its easy figure.
A stillness greatens, in which

The whole house seems to be thinking,
And then she is at it again with a bunched clamor
Of strokes, and again is silent.

I remember the dazed starling
Which was trapped in that very room, two years ago;
How we stole in, lifted a sash

And retreated, not to affright it;
And how for a helpless hour, through the crack of the door,
We watched the sleek, wild, dark

And iridescent creature
Batter against the brilliance, drop like a glove
To the hard floor, or the desk-top,

And wait then, humped and bloody,
For the wits to try it again; and how our spirits
Rose when, suddenly sure,

It lifted off from a chair-back
Beating a smooth course for the right window
And clearing the sill of the world.

It is always a matter, my darling,
Of life or death, as I had forgotten. I wish
What I wished you before, but harder.

—Richard Wilbur

Wilbur's poem is accentual—three stresses apiece in the first and third lines of each stanza, and five apiece in the middle lines—but I haven't chosen it to discuss meter. Rather, I'd like to look at how it begins, continues, and ends.

That's a simple enough first line, isn't it? Anyone can write that, right? Imagine yourself writing it: "In her room at the front of the house. . . ." No, not "front," but "prow." One word has been changed in a phrase anyone might utter over coffee or on the telephone. Instead of "her room at the front of the house," Wilbur says, "at the *prow* of the house."

Why? Well, any reason will do, and it's possible that the poet simply thought to jazz it up a bit, to be figurative because poetry thrives on figurative language and because this poet has a talent for making figures. It's even possible that the poet's house somehow resembles a boat. My own suspicion is that this is simply one more example of a poet using what comes to mind. Wilbur is a sailor; he served in the Navy; he vacations in Key West on the Atlantic. To him it must be natural to identify the front of a house with the prow of a boat.

Lines two and three announce the place and the plot. What could be more straightforward? "My daughter is writing a story." And what could be more natural but that the proud father, a writer himself, pause in the stairwell to listen? He stands outside her door and hears the sound of typing, and how does he describe it? First, as "a commotion of typewriter-keys." That's more figure-making, at first blush an elementary sort, the kind of prepositional phrase figure-making we were asked to compose on the blackboard in grade school—an "enigma of elephants," and so forth—except that this one contains nothing made-up. What he hears is, in fact, a noisy commotion, in which the clamor of the keys also signals the creative turmoil taking place in her room.

Here Wilbur decides to extend the figure with a simile. Well, a poem must listen to itself and give visible indications of listening to itself. Hence, having likened the front of the house to the prow of a boat, he chooses another nautical item to which to liken the sound of the typewriter: the sound of a chain being hauled over a gunwale. Is she, perhaps, pulling up anchor?

Likewise, stanza three is witty and showy. If the house is a ship, why then her life in it carries cargo, some of it heavy, and one may wish her a lucky passage—both in her story and on the sea of life. That's easy: serious but easy.

The poem is still listening—rereading—itself. And what has it heard so far? It has heard a proud father saying the usual things, albeit with grace and flair. And so we come to the second part of this poem, in which the father will realize how casually one may wish someone good luck. Please notice, by the way, that he didn't write, "But now it is she who pauses, to reject my thought and its easy figure." No, that would have been mere fancy. He can't know what the silence means, and so he writes, ". . . as *if* to reject my thought and its easy figure." His simile was an easy figure for her typing; his metaphor was an easy figure for her writing and her life; *he* is, likewise, an easy figure pausing for a moment outside her door, calm against the clamor of her keys.

At this point in the poem, it might seem that there is nothing further to say, at least not if one is able to resist the siren call of one's abstract ideas and bald statements of feeling. It is time to look elsewhere, and the poet looks, as poets will, into memory. For when the poem listens to itself, the poet has been listening to *himself or herself*, and listening to oneself is listening to the past. Language can eat the future, but it lives off the past.

He remembers a trapped bird—in that very room—who had to try and try. When it fell, he tells us, it fell "like a glove," sometimes to the "desk-top," and one may picture the writer's hand slumping from the keys to the desk in between sentences. But there is more to the parallel. The bird grew humped and bloody in its effort. Its success in getting out of that room depended on its wits, or brains, and it had to learn the hard way on its own.

Finally, it makes it, "clearing the sill of the . . . window." No, the "sill of the *world*." If we didn't get it, we do now: his daughter's writing a story is part of her growing up and away. She, too, will someday clear the sill of their world: the world of the family and of her room at the prow of the house.

Guess what? This is serious business after all. The triumph of this poem, the big thing which depends on all the little things along the way, lies in the speaker, the father, taking his daughter more and more seriously. Finally, he says it: "It is always a matter, my darling,/ of life or death, as I had forgotten. I wish/what I wished you before, but harder." One thing that poems do is to give a phrase or sentence or thought more meaning. Or to find out how much more it meant all along. "I wish what I wished you before, but harder."

When I reread this poem, I see many reassuring things for a writer. I see that simple details can have meaning beyond furnishing a world or telling a story. I see that the past may relate to the present and vice versa. I see that what begins in word-play may end in honor. I see again how the very essence of a poem may be to arrive at that spot at which the speaker may call his daughter his darling.

Okay, that's groundwork. How is my reading of it affected by my being a writer? Primarily, in this way: having read it and been taken by the reality and clarity of its feelings, I go back to see how the poem might have been written. I try to imagine myself freely arriving at the same words, images, associations, and thoughts, in the same order.

You know, it's a truism that one learns to write by reading. But not necessarily by *wide* reading. Rather, by *deep* reading. One might read a few things over and over, perhaps over a period of years, and so be more lastingly influenced than by a slighter acquaintance with more.

Of course one may read and reread happily without thinking about it, learning by intuition, and certainly some poems are less discussable than others. I have a theory—just one of many theories that come and go, depending on the context—that the great achievements of American poetry have been essentially those of rhetoric rather than of image and metaphor, or of imagination, structure, and vision. In American poetry, as you all know, great emphasis has been placed on an individual tone of voice. The great Mommas and Daddies of modern poetry in English are enormously distinctive, each from the others. The great flowering of American poets mainly born in the twenties exhibits individuality of style and of tone of voice in profusion. From the late 1950s until the late 1960s, it seemed as if few American poets wanted to look or sound as if they had anything in common. The goal was an individual voice, and I suspect that retrospective analysis will find the content far less individuated than the variety of styles implied. Nonetheless, the Imagists had said that a new cadence meant a new idea—essentially a defense of formalism, whether in traditional forms, variants of them, or so-called free verse. Not a new imagination, mind you, a new *idea*. The emphasis on ideas, baldly stated or only insinuated, in American poetry has meant an emphasis on those aspects of a poem that are essentially rhetorical. The secrets of tone are, for the most part, those of syntax and words without meaning, so-called "function words" that indicate relationships: subordination, coordination, conjunction, opposition, etc. Syntax is logic, or the appearance of it, and new logic inevitably produces a new tone of voice.

In the classroom, we tend to marvel at rhetoric, and to discuss most freely poems held together by rhetoric, poems in which, however frontal the narrative, however rich in objects, images, or metaphors, however insistent in vision, the poem is primarily a set of rhetorical maneuvers.

It is harder, much harder, to learn from poems that skip that rhetorical level and that present themselves as associational texts in which the reasoning is in between the lines while the lines themselves present only the emblems of experience and, sometimes, of epiphany.

### To the Saguaro Cactus Tree in the Desert Rain

I had no idea the elf owl
Crept into you in the secret
Of night.

I have torn myself out of many bitter places
In America, that seemed
Tall and green-rooted in mid-noon.
I wish I were the spare shadow
Of the roadrunner, I wish I were
The honest lover of the diamondback
And the tear the tarantula weeps.

I had no idea you were so tall
And blond in moonlight.

I got thirsty in the factories,
And I hated the brutal dry suns there,
So I quit.

You were the shadow
Of a hallway
In me.

I have never gone through that door,
But the elf owl's face
Is inside me.

Saguaro,
You are not one of the gods.
Your green arms lower and gather me.
I am an elf owl's shadow, a secret
Member of your family.

—James Wright

James Wright's poem may seem "farther out" than Wilbur's "The Writer." Its images seem to lie on the page as if disconnected, each from each. If by rhetoric the poem establishes its tone of voice and hints at connections, nowhere do we come on anything as bald as, "It is always a matter, my darling, of life or death, as I had forgotten." Instead we get, "I have never gone through that door,/But the elf owl's face/Is inside me."

Now look again at the first three lines. From the writer's point of view—that is, from the point of view of a thief—what's to notice? The basic sentence is a simple statement of fact: the elf owl creeps into the saguaro at night. But Wright says "secret" of night. "Secret" is one of James Wright's special words. It shows up often in his last three books. From its recurrent use we can tell that it holds symbolic and visionary overtones for him, much as "grace," "noon," "seal," "purple," and "circumference" held for Emily Dickinson. From the canon of Wright's poetry we can tell that his use of the word "secret" comes from his feeling that a man's life is inside him, out of view of others, not one's public life at all—something private, personal, and intimate. But of course you don't have to know any of that. The phrase here, "secret of night," makes perfect sense all by itself. Night is the great cover. The elf owl *creeps* secretively into the tree.

The other tiny "extra" in what would otherwise be a plain sentence of desert lore is the rhetorical maneuver at the start: "I had no idea." That's immediate involvement; the voice of the poem is at once strong and engaged. A stance has been taken. While such small maneuvers may come to be second nature, using them is quite as much a matter of technique as is calling a section of one's house by the name for a section of a boat.

From here on, the poem will increasingly identify with the elf owl. Wright says that he has had to tear himself away from many places that seemed to be, like the cactus tree that is home to the elf owl, tall and green-rooted. But, being a man, he wasn't able to live in a cactus tree. His desert was that of the factories where he worked and quit.

Still, there is in each of us a secret life. A life in which we identify with the elf owl, and in which we see ourselves living at night in a cactus tree in the welcome desert rain. And so he says, addressing the tree, "You were the shadow/Of a hallway/In me." If, being a man, he has never gone through that door, at least he can say of himself that he carries the elf owl's face inside.

The poem listens to itself. That is how it arrives at tall and green-rooted places in mid-noon, to echo and parallel a cactus tree in the desert. That is how it finds its way to factories which are themselves scorched deserts.

But the poem does not merely repeat itself. Try out the last stanza without its second line. Without "You are not one of the gods," it would simply be more of the same. What has been added? For one thing, in case the reader was wondering—no, he is not according the tree divinity. Moreover, the line contains a certain insistence on facts and this world, the sort of insistence we saw four lines earlier when he said, "I have never gone through that door." Without such moves, a poem is limited to mere fancy: a story, say, about a man who could live inside a cactus and talk to elf owls. No; it is not a story at all, but an expression of a secret identification and a longing to be naturally at home.

From the very first, this poem held my interest as a writer. James Wright began writing poetry as a formalist, indebted to the poems of Edwin Arlington Robinson. With *The Branch Will Not Break*, his poetry underwent a sea change, apparently influenced by his reading and translating of Spanish poets and the German expressionist poet Georg Trakl. Thereafter, Wright was always said to be a surrealistic image-maker. In later books, he put back the open-faced rhetoric he had forsaken in *The Branch Will Not Break*, but he continued to compose, also, great flourishes of surrealistic imagery. In this poem to the saguaro, the landscape takes on a surreal tinge—it helps in the desert to be among The Friends of Salvador Dali—but it is not fanciful. Everything here is real.

We should all, I would think, wish to write such lines as, "You were the shadow/Of a hallway/In me," and, "I am an elf owl's shadow, a secret/Member of your family." It may help, therefore, to notice how Wright gets to such lines and why they hold such meaning when he does. You don't come to, "You were the *shadow* of a hallway in me," unless you first see in the cactus tree a hallway for an elf owl. One of the things poems do is to add meaning to what has already been said: "I wish what I wished you before, but harder."

Now pause a moment over the last two lines of the poem. There are the words "shadow" and "secret" again. Are they just vague emotional equivalents to the speaker's feelings, or do they make sense based on what "shadow" and "secret" meant when he used them earlier? See if you agree with this logic: if the cactus tree was a hallway to the elf owl in the desert, and was therefore the shadow of a hallway to the worker in the hot factories, then the worker could become the shadow of the elf owl. Each is a part of the other. The elf owl doesn't live exclusively in the cool tree, but also in the burning desert. Indeed, he "creeps" into the tree, a secret act in the night. Nor does the worker's entire life take place in the brutal light of factories. He has his naturally cool places, his secret life. The living elf owl and the living man are one, more so than the speaker realized, perhaps, when he wished openly to be the shadow of the roadrunner, the lover of the diamondback, and the tear wept by the tarantula. He is, in a sense, all of those—the more so if he knows it. If the green arms of the saguaro do not lower and gather him *in fact*, in his mind he is able to rise to embrace them and to affirm his identification with the world and all its forms of life.

Sometimes, at the end of a poem, the world is larger, and the speaker is less alone.

James Wright also wrote short pieces in paragraphs. He explained that he "wanted to learn to write prose." Are they prose, or prose poetry, or are they poems that happen to have been set down in paragraphs? I would say that it is a sign of the times—some would say a bad sign, others would say a good sign—that we need not linger on the question. Our technical definitions and technical standards for poetry have been greatly enriched by a larger, untechnical understanding based on the quality of the poetic imagination, and on what we might call "poetic structure": how the poem proceeds from one thing to another and how meaning is apprehended, enlarged, or diminished.

Our American poetry and the ways in which we speak about it have been changed since the mid-1960s, perhaps not as much by the examples of our own best poets, or by those who have been brought to our shores from other English-speaking countries aboard barrages of publicity, as by poetry in translation. These changes were not wrought only by the finest, most considered, and most accurate translations (for example, Mark Strand's versions of Alberti and Andrade, or Charles Simic's of Vasko Popa, or Alistair Reid's of Pablo Neruda, or translations of Zbigniew Herbert by Czeslaw Milosz and Peter Dale Scott, or those of Cavafy by Edmund Keeley and George Savidis). They came about also because of those translations that, like Ezra Pound's of Li Po, take liberties with the literal and with form to render, perhaps even to exaggerate, the spirit of the poem (for example, Robert Bly's versions of Neruda, Lorca, Jiménez, Rumi, Rilke, Martinson, Ekelof, and Tranströmer, and W. S. Merwin's translations from both eastern and western languages). And there were the best of the anthologies of poetry in translation (of which I will mention Mark Strand and Charles Simic's *Another Republic*, Czeslaw Milosz's *Postwar Polish Poetry*, Hardie St. Martin's *Roots and Wings: Poetry from Spain, 1900–1975*, and that hoary old favorite, perhaps now forgotten, Robert Payne's anthology of

Chinese poetry, *The White Pony*, first published in 1947 and again in 1960). But it was not only the finest translations, nor the most accurate, nor the most conscious of spirit and imagination, nor the best anthologies that influenced us to think more broadly about poetry, but so also random translations by poets who did merely a little of this or that, using a "pony" and a dictionary to translate a few Persian ghazals or one or two poems by the Spanish poet Unamuno, say.

In every translation, there comes to us a new wave of permission, an increased sense of freedom. Is it because we are forced to abandon our prejudices and preferences if we are to enjoy travel? Is it because not all cultures share our overwhelmingly technical view of things? Is it because the pressures of empire, even a crumbling empire involved in a desperate holding action, affect our point of view? No doubt it is for all these reasons and others. One thing is certain: every literature has grown fresh, and every great writer been made greater, by writers looking to other cultures and languages for new words and renewed permission.

So, if we look at a short poem by Tomas Tranströmer, translated from the Swedish, we have to adjust our way of learning.

### After a Death

Once there was a shock
that left behind a long, shimmering comet tail.
It keeps us inside. It makes the TV pictures snowy.
It settles in cold drops on the telephone wires.

One can still go slowly on skis in the winter sun
through brush where a few leaves hang on.
They resemble pages torn from old telephone directories.
Names swallowed by the cold.

It is still beautiful to feel the heart beat
but often the shadow seems more real than the body.
The samurai looks insignificant
beside his armor of black dragon scales.

—Tomas Tranströmer
tr. by Robert Bly

The poem is titled "After a Death." One could easily misremember it as "After a Shock," for that is how it feels. It is not an elegy. We are told nothing about the person who has died, not even his name. We read only that the death was indeed a shock. There is a mention of television. Perhaps it was someone famous. Perhaps it was an assassination. Perhaps it was the killing of John F. Kennedy. In fact, it was. Tranströmer says so. But I note that he does not say so in the poem nor even offer a dedication or an epigraph in memoriam. The poem is more general than that. Tranströmer says that an uncle died around the same time, and that the deaths combine in the poem. In my mind, I contrast his way with the sometimes unseemly American rush to dedicate poems, to mention the names of famous friends, and to publish elegies for poets before the ink has dried on their obits.

Of course, the rush to identify and dedicate is not born of bad intentions. We want everything to be particular. We love particulars. We have faith in particulars. We honestly believe that, if we can get the particulars correct and in the right order, our job will be done and the poem will be complete.

Perhaps we favor particulars in part because our choice has long seemed to lie exclusively between specifics and explanation. For important reasons, we favor the concrete over the abstract, the particular over the general, presentation over explanation, showing over telling.

Yet so much poetry from other cultures exhibits both the tensile strength of the particular and the active force of the general. How does this happen?

I can spot elements in this Tranströmer poem that line up with the question. Conventionally, we can say that a long, shimmering comet tail is a fine metaphor for the sudden, fiery grief that exploded when Kennedy was assassinated and then streaked into darkness. Or for any death that comes as a shock. But I notice, also, the first thing, which is simply the poet's leap into the heavens and then his sudden drop back to earth and the domestic: "It keeps us inside," a wonderful detail; "It makes the TV pictures snowy." Do these things feel right? Obviously. Do they make sense physically? Yes, for a comet tail might be thought to affect electronic reception. If it's exaggeration, it only imitates in hyperbole the extreme emotions of shock and grief. And the fourth line—"It settles in cold drops on the telephone wires"—continues the images of difficult communication, messages, all in the air. If the telephone lines themselves sweat cold beads, what effect must the news be having on human beings?

Some kind of thinking has taken place between stanzas one and two. I can imagine it. While the poet was asking himself, unconsciously, "What next?" for his poem, he came to the same question about his subject. For there is nothing notable to say about the anatomy and biology of death which would advance this poem. The rest of the event is only news.

This is another way in which a poem can listen to itself. The poem does not listen to itself merely so that it can gain applause by showing that it did. No, it listens for clues. "What next?" Imagine this. You are sitting at your kitchen table, writing. You have written four lines. You read those four lines as if you were someone other than the writer, someone who asks a question or disagrees. Now you know what to say next.

After a shocking death, one can still go out into the same world, on skis if you are in the right place and season for them, but the world will seem changed. The few leaves hanging from winter brush will resemble pages. And here we notice something having perhaps no basis in the original language of the poem: that the English plural of "leaf" is "leaves." But pages of what? The poem is still paying attention to itself. Remember those telephone wires in line four? "Pages torn from old telephone directories"; hence, "names swallowed by the cold." Cold drops on the wires, names swallowed by the cold, a lump in the throat—as separate as the images may seem when we first come upon them, they live in one neighborhood.

The beginning of the final stanza of this poem reminds me of the distance between our poets and many of our critics. Few of our critics would care for a line like, "It is still beautiful to feel the heart beat." Half of our poets and most of our critics write as if they believe that, since life ends in death, we are essentially dead. Hence, they believe, sometimes without knowing it, that *any* uncomplicated emotion about life is excessive: therefore, sentimental. But poetry, because it is written by the living to be read by the living, is a way of *life*. It is always about *living*, even in the shadow of death. The samurai's armor of black dragon scales, which Tranströmer saw in the Stockholm Museum, overshadows the swordsman, and the shadow often "seems more real than the body," but it is "still beautiful to feel the heart beat." Without line nine, the poem would be different. Without line nine, it would not be wisdom, but complaint.

Now, this Tranströmer poem, in translation, does not show a certain vibrancy of language American poetry readers favor, nor a fiercely idiomatic character, nor a sharply etched individual tone. It comes to us in a neutral tone, in an almost impersonal voice, yet I find in it a certain intimacy regardless—perhaps because of the very objects in the poem (TV, telephone, brush, and leaves), and perhaps because it asks the question most of *us* would ask, "What next?" And perhaps simply because it employs the word "us."

And it accomplishes extra meaning in its last sentence, just as the Wilbur and Wright poems did. That the suit of armor dwarfs the samurai might be merely a museum fact, something which moves us to say, "Look at that!" Occurring where it does in the poem, however, we are more likely to say, "*Think* about that!" Thus, the writer has taken a detail from a museum display and, by a deft use of context, set free an emotional weight it always contained. I find this quality in poetry from other countries more often than in American poems: the quality, that is, of releasing from objects the emotional force they hold in quiet.

Now I'd like to strengthen or weaken my case, and add a dimension to it, by confessing that I sometimes read, in private, my own poems. And that I read them the same way—to see, as much as possible, how they were written.

You might think I ought to have known everything at the time, but what we first do consciously later becomes second nature, and I believe in any case in inspiration, spontaneity, association, accident, and temporary insanity. During the interminable time of a writing block, I am tempted to employ a rubber stamp reading, "Temporarily Deceased."

Here, then, is another poem subject to rereading, just as if it were someone else's.

### To an Adolescent Weeping Willow

I don't know what you think you're doing,
sweeping the ground. You
do it so easily, backhanded, forehanded.
You hardly bend. Really, you sway.

What can it mean
when a thing is so easy?

I threw dirt on my father's floor.
Not dirt, but a chopped green
dirt which picked up dirt.

I pushed the pushbroom.
I oiled the wooden floor of the store.

He bent over and lifted the coal
into the coal stove. With the back of the shovel
he came down on the rat just topping the bin
and into the fire.

What do you think?—Did he sway?
Did he kiss a rock for luck?
Did he soak up water
and climb into light and turn and turn?

Did he weep and weep in the yard?

Yes, I think he did. Yes,
now I think he did.

So, Willow, you come sweep my floor.
I have no store.
I have a yard. A big yard.

I have a song to weep.
I have a cry.

You who rose up from the dirt,
because I put you there
and like to walk my head in under
your earliest feathery branches—
what can it mean
when a thing is so easy?

It means you are a boy.

Right away, I notice things. It seems to me that this poet began
with a line that is both sincere and tricky. He challenged the tree.
Even before he told us one thing about it, he got worked up. Im-
mediate emotion. Condition *now*. A rhetorical maneuver, cast in the
idiomatic language of ordinary people, perhaps similar to the first
sentences of certain favorite poems by James Wright: "The Old WPA
Swimming Pool in Martins Ferry, Ohio," for example, which begins,
"I am almost afraid/To write down/This thing." Or, "To the Saguaro
Cactus Tree in the Desert Rain," which begins, "I had no *idea*. . . ."
Influence? More accurately, something of experience and language
held in common and welcomed into the writing because one has seen
it employed elsewhere.

I can hear the poem listening to itself, using the rest of the first
stanza to explain the challenge of the first line. And I can see, now,
that the poet simply turned his back on the question he had posed:
"What can it mean/when a thing is so easy?"

Even that little bit of evidence suggests that the poem is not about what the speaker knows as much as it is about what he doesn't yet know he knows. And to find out what one doesn't know one knows, one must sometimes look elsewhere. It's a process that happens when you go to bed to sleep on a problem and wake with the answer. Physicists do it all the time. Freud did it. Does it matter *where* one looks while looking away? I tend to think not. The self has a coherence, and the poet, good or lucky or both, can retrace those connections later on.

Looking back, it all seems patently obvious. The willow stands swaying easily in dirt. The speaker in the poem (the poet, yes) once did something involving dirt that was easy to do but that now seems, at first glance, to have contained the seeds of unease—so much so that the poet immediately retreats to explain. He wasn't bad, he didn't make trouble for his father; he was good, he helped.

In fact, he did more. He swept up, and he oiled the floor.

"Yes," says that invisible reader, lurking behind the writer's shoulder (though never in the direction in which the writer looks). "Yes, but what did *he* do while you were handling your childhood chores? Didn't he do the harder things? Let's name a couple to remind you."

And that's enough of *that*. Is this a poem about running a five-and-ten? No, we don't know what it's going to be about—mostly, finally—but it won't be that. "Don't forget," says the second self, "you're talking to a tree. You asked it a question, so far unanswered. Can you answer it or not? Not yet? Then why not ask the tree some more questions?" *Hotshot tree, doing everything so easily. . . . Do you think my father was like you? Did he sway, kiss a rock, soak up water and climb into light?* And now comes a lucky moment in the language. It's not just any old tree; it's a willow, a *weeping* willow. "Did he weep and weep in the yard?" That means one thing for the tree and another for one's father. Asked about a tree, it's a piece of light wit, but it's damn serious when asked about the father.

Suddenly, the poet is forced to answer his own seemingly rhetorical questions. When he began questioning the tree in earnest, they were questions that seemed to suggest differences. One expected them to be answered with "no's," but it turns out the answer was "yes" all along, even in a sense to the first and last question.

So now the weeping willow—at the start, bothersome, even offensive, in its ease—can be accepted. The poet has asked his challenging question and, though he has yet to answer it, has bled the confusion and confrontation from it. The willow and his father have much in common.

The differences, however, are still at issue. *Willow, come sweep my floor. I have no store, but I have a yard. I do the father's singing and crying now. Not only that, I planted you there.*

What, then, of the question posed in lines five and six: "What can it mean when a thing is so easy?" Looking back at this poem, trying to imagine myself at the time of writing it, it seems to me that by writing the poem I found the answer—to what *I* meant, not to what the same question might mean when asked by one of you. The question itself had to be given more meaning by the poem, meaning that lurked underneath when the poem began.

It takes the whole poem to answer the question. Then it takes only one sentence of six monosyllabic words to deliver the answer. The willow is an adolescent. That is why some things are easy for it. Moreover, the seeming ease of youth is characteristic of the distance in time between any father and any son, not the distance of not getting along but the distance of cold fact: the son knows little of the consciousness of the father. The son hangs around, sweeps the floor. He assumes life feels more or less the same for his father, who fires the coal stove and kills rats in the basement. He doesn't know, like they say, shit. Not because he is stupid or unsympathetic. His not knowing means only that he is a boy, not a man. He will know the difference when he is a man.

I am reassured when I look again at this poem. It says to me that I can pose a question and not answer it while the poem goes on, confident that an answer will arrive. It says to me that I can talk to one person (or a tree) about another. I see, as I have always suspected, that I feel a heightened engagement when I address someone or some thing directly—that, in that sense, I want the poem to matter because someone is listening. I see that, when I ask a question, I want it to be answered. I suspect that I could derive from this poem a method by which to write others. The method would require a challenging remark, some description of what is being addressed, a question to be answered at the end, and a set of memories set down one after another until a connection has been achieved between memory and the thing being addressed, acceptance has replaced the initial challenge, and a resolution occurs. I am not interested in applying such a method myself, if it *is* one, but I see that it might be done, and that something similar might be done out of any poem that interests one enough. I know of one poet who writes her poems primarily by extrapolating requirements from other people's poems. After all, one's own obsessions and language will surface regardless.

In conclusion, I'd like to talk about what it takes besides talent and perseverance to make the big leagues. Everyone knows that, no matter how good you are in your hometown, at some point you have got to play with and against the best. If your kid is really that talented with the violin, he or she needs a world-class teacher. It's no accident that a large number of the best basketball players in the country come from a few well-known schools and playgrounds, or that hotshot high school baseball and tennis players head for those particular warm climates where the other hotshots have gone. Louis Armstrong and Miles Davis didn't get to play that way by stepping on the football field with the high school band to play marches. You want to be a carpenter, you've got to apprentice yourself to a good one. You want to be a tailor, it helps to know at least one person who can make a suit.

Well, one can't always give up everything and go off to hang around the right playground or teacher. But in literature it's different: one *can* hang out with the best. It's all right there in the library.

Still, the books are not the process. What's in the books is the end result. It's as if one saw the ball going through the basket again and again, without ever seeing the moves that made the shot possible. Consequently, if you are to learn from what is given you, the poem itself, you must put yourself into it again and again, imagining the process—nay, *inventing* the process—by which the poem may have come to be. More often than not, what you invent will be sort of what the poet did.

From rereading, you will grow up and go free. Then, getting your poems written will depend on need, luck, and perseverance. The rest is genius.

# Noun/Object/Image

W E are greedy. We want the image to be more than the object, despite how hard it is merely to see an object and render it accurately. We are self-centered. We want the image to be partly subjective. We are proud. We want the image to carry our "vision." We are vain and competitive. We want the image to be *our* kind of image, *our* signature, *our* brick wall.

But photographers can do the object, and painters redo it, better than we. What can we do with it that they cannot?

We can put the object into motion, a motion even more continuous than that of moving pictures, where the screen must stay out. We can give the image a nonimagistic context. Hence, the object alone will suffice if by itself it contains inside and outside, self and other, here and there. Of course, we can also make of the image a place. We can locate there. And we can use the image to objectify our emotions, even sometimes to express them.

Most of the talk about imagery sounds like broadcasts of Army football games of the forties. Mr. Inside and Mr. Outside (Doc Blanchard and Glenn Davis), working together, couldn't be beat. And it's true that a star or two will compensate for one's deficiencies elsewhere. In our time, an ordinary mind with a talent for vivid imagery is probably more likely to be praised than is a brilliant mind lacking it. We are not just tv watchers. We have become tv readers.

Pound's definition of the image—"an intellectual and emotional complex in an instant of time" (*Poetry*, March 1913)—is often reduced in conversation about the image. For all his learning, Pound's heart remained in popular song—Provençal lyrics. He would never have made poetry by squeezing it just from his brain, as have his more esoteric followers.

Pound's image has two parts, and produces an equation between feeling and object. Stieglitz was making such an equation when he photographed clouds and called them "equivalents." The clouds were equivalent to his emotions. No emotions, no images.

Imagism, remember, in reaction to the second-best poetry of its time, published a complete set of principles for poetry writing. Its advice to show, not tell, was only a part of its program. When it turned into what E. P. called "Amygism" (for Amy Lowell)—poetry that imitated the method without emotional depth—Pound got out.

Now, the image doesn't work the way we say it does. Take probably the two best-known examples of Imagism. First, Pound's "In a Station of the Metro." Pound finds it necessary to use half the poem to explain what's coming: "The apparition of these faces in the crowd." Only then can he lay before us an image: "Petals on a wet, black bough." The poem accomplishes an image, but not without explanation.

Second, Williams' "The Red Wheelbarrow." "So much depends," he writes, "upon/a red wheel/barrow," and then says nothing about what depends on it. The poem argues for Imagism, but its method is rhetorical: the effect of the poem *depends* on the rhetorical beginning of its only sentence to establish expectation and then frustrate it. Pulling the rug out from under the reader, it makes its point by saying no more. In other words, though one could argue the propriety and advantages of having the object be a red wheelbarrow, it could have been something else.

Are the greatest accomplishments of American poetry those of imagery? I myself think not. American poetry tends to be heavy on rhetoric but light on imagery. Indeed, the colloquialization of rhetoric may be an American accomplishment. The British are better in court, but their poetic rhetoric wears leaden boots. The French do more acrobatics, but say less. Our idiomatic lingo is heavily rhetorical and metaphorical.

Our practice of Imagism (I would argue that we have been practicing at it ever since the Movement) much of the time has been mindless—the one aspect of American poetry that most reveals our poetics to be limited by an absence of sufficiently considered theory.

Of course, my ideas about imagery have in some ways changed and in others remained constant, just as I have changed and remained constant. I don't usually think about imagery apart from other concerns. Still, I tend to think of our preoccupation with images as characteristic of our technological society. I am fairly sure that images in poems have less effect and less value than is claimed by those who are dependent upon them. I know that imagery can be a breeding ground for the fraudulent visionary, the mystifier. I suspect imagery has kept many unthinking poets writing and publishing, but there's always something.

Those among us who love Imagism are held back by its dead hand. So are those of us who hate it. To be free, one must proceed as if writing is an adventure into the unknown. From the beginning, one may see or imagine many images. And later there may be many surprises, some of which may also be images. The "so much" that "depends" on each object/image is the object/image itself. In a field, we too are among those objects. The notion that a man or woman's brain is superior to a tree will lead to the premature end of civilization. But so will the notion that a tree is superior to a brain. At least the tree, as far as we can tell, is too smart to think so.

Now if we take up the poetry of William Carlos Williams, one of the most misunderstood, mislabeled, and poorly imitated poets of our time (still!), we shall never see the end of our discussion. For Williams is a poet of syntax and idea far more than he is a poet of things or images. His "thing" poems are mere exercises. His great works are not at all dependent on batches of images. Rather, like most great poems, they are each centered in one image—an image from which the poem derives, or toward which it proceeds. The image of the *poem* is vastly more important than the image in the *line*.

My book titles are images, but not always things. Is this possible? I think so. The titles are *Things We Dreamt We Died For*; *A Probable Volume of Dreams*; *The Escape into You*; *Residue of Song*; *Stars Which See, Stars Which Do Not See*; *These Green-Going-to-Yellow*; *Drawn by Stones, by Earth, by Things That Have Been in the Fire*; *Old Snow Just Melting*; *Iris of Creation*; and *The Book of the Dead Man*. None displays a single object to which a reader might attach his or her understanding of the entire phrase. I would hope that each image is larger than that. To my way of thinking, an object that has been turned on its head or covered with a shroud is still just an object. In such cases, one tends to turn it right-side-up or uncover it in one's mind, thus enjoying the pleasure of a riddle. For me, however, writing is not riddling, any more than the unexplored polar cap was a riddle for Byrd. Call it a riddle, if you like; it was a great space.

In my generation, the best image makers include Mark Strand, Charles Simic, Louise Glück, and Charles Wright. In the generation ahead of mine, one would have to name Galway Kinnell and James Wright. In the poetry of James Wright, we can trace the development of what is best in American poetic imagery. In mid-career, by way of Spanish and German poets (notably, Trakl), he develops the some-times startling, subjective imagery of *The Branch Will Not Break*. But imagery is not enough, so he puts back more rhetoric in *Shall We Gather at the River*. In the end, in *To a Blossoming Pear Tree*, he writes a plain, colloquial, narrative line, made glorious, heightened, and also relieved by gorgeous images—many of them emotional cor-relatives, not to what has already been expressed outright, or will be, but to other, deeper responses. In such work, Wright refines one of the most powerful uses of the image (to tell us something more, from underneath) and also implies by his continuing need for rhetoric the limits of the image (for the "deep" image, once allowed to dominate the surface of the poem, becomes only the surface).

Images are not the essence of poetry, even for those who have a talent for them. They are only one among many symptoms of a poet's quality of mind and force of imagination. Still, I too am knocked out by them. Who would not wish to have written these lines by Theodore Roethke: "Is that dance slowing in the mind of man/That made him think the universe could hum?" I myself see an image at their center. I also think an image is contained in these lines: "The rain/is too heavy a whistle for the certainty of charity." Those are my own lines, and they have haunted me for years.

The image is bigger than the object. But the noun is larger still. The secrets of the mind take the form of nouns. Those images in dreams that are taken to signify: they are merely the surface of things.

# Three Propositions: Hooey,
# Dewey, and Loony

I H A V E brought something along to serve as prologue. It's an article by Bob Thomas of Associated Press in which Thomas is interviewing William Shatner about the movie "Star Trek V: The Final Frontier." This is not the first occasion on which William Shatner, better known as Captain Kirk of the Starship Enterprise, has spoken for me. You may remember that, in "Star Trek IV: The Voyage Home," Captain Kirk and his crew return to Earth in our time. Kirk is eating pizza in a joint in San Francisco with a woman whose help he will need, when he decides to fess up about who he is and where he has come from. The camera circles the room, then homes in on Kirk and his companion as she bursts out with, "YOU MEAN YOU'RE FROM OUTER SPACE?" "No," says Kirk, "I'm from Iowa. I only *work* in outer space."

That was the first time that the Captain spoke for me. The second time occurs in this article. Trying to explain the popularity of "Star Trek," Kirk—I mean, Shatner—says: "Is it possible that we're creating a mythology? . . . The more I read and the more I think about it, I wonder if the key to 'Star Trek' is not all the wonderful stuff we talk about: the character interplay, the sci-fi, action and adventure and all those good things that seem to be on the surface. Somewhere underneath, the chemistry and the concept touch upon a mythological need in modern culture. That's my real thought." And then he backs up just like a writer and says, "I don't quite know what I mean. It would take a far more intelligent and perceptive person to divine what I mean."

Since we are free in the imagination to begin anywhere, let me begin with three propositions about poets. The first is an analysis in the form of a prediction, the second is an explanation, and the third is a testimonial. Here are the three propositions: (1) The future belongs to the helpless; (2) we all think we are frauds but none of us is rich enough to say so in public; and (3) the rain is too heavy a whistle for the certainty of charity.

First, "the future belongs to the helpless." I phrased it thus to echo the confidence with which the Russian poet Yevgeny Yevtushenko some years ago proclaimed that in poetry the future belonged to those poets who could jump the farthest, those who could freely associate most wildly. Although at the time Russian and East European writers often spoke about politics in unpolitical metaphors— hence, a Polish pencil might stand for a Polish bureaucrat—the "free association" to which Yevtushenko was referring was not the coming liberalism of *perestroika*, but that of juxtaposition, which, it can be argued, may be poetry's most constant and visible technique.

But what does one mean by a "constant, visible technique?" First, we have to make some gesture toward defining a playing field where any technique might matter. So here is today's definition of poetry. It has occurred to me, during the ongoing game—and it is only a game: artificial in conception, justified by assumptions, dependent on tacit cooperation, and well forgotten afterwards—the game of defining poetry, vis-à-vis prose, that we might say that prose is prose because of what it includes while poetry is poetry because of what it leaves out.

Juxtaposition is a form of leaving out. Pound wanted more of it, demonstrating its strength in his broad editing of "The Wasteland." In its simplest manifestation, it means leaving out the transitions. The practice overlaps the classroom advice to "Show, don't tell," it reiterates by example Archibald MacLeish's well-known line, "A poem should not mean, but be," and it reaffirms Billie Holiday's "Don't explain."

Why should a poem be effective, even "poetic," because it leaves things out? Shouldn't a reader—intelligent, practical, demanding, sensible, reasonable—want to secure a path through the poem at first glance? Whoa! I have imagined a reader who isn't necessarily a reader of poetry. A reader of poetry, while reading, is not practical, but indulgent; not demanding, but attentive; not sensible, but audacious; not reasonable, but imaginative; not even as much intelligent as simply aware. For poetry, like beauty, is in the eye of the beholder. One cannot make an unwilling reader see the unflowering life of a poem when he or she has something else to do, such as proving a point.

The action of poetry requires a reader. The writer, having found his or her way from the first word of the poem to the last, leaves it to the reader to find the route for himself or herself. Each rereading is a fresh start. As for the Emily Dickinsons of this world, publishing little or not at all during their lifetimes, they must be their own and perhaps only readers, but so are we all as we write and then first see what it is we have written.

Poetry is unparaphraseable. We repeat this maxim, we shove it in the faces of critics, we use it to escape the responsibility of the classroom, and we are allowed to because, yes, it is true. The Imagist Credo: A new cadence is a new idea. Robert Creeley, as quoted by Charles Olson: "Form is never more than an extension of content." Frank Lloyd Wright: "Form follows function." How a poem says what it says *is* what it says. We all know this. Of course, no word expresses what another word expresses, we all know this too (there are no absolute synonyms), and this truth is promoted by the phrase and further by the sentence and so is true of all language. In poetry, however, it is true with a vengeance. To apprehend the full expression that is a poem, we have to read between the lines, go outside the borders, engage in metaphor, hear the silences, change direction in the interludes, and, often most importantly, be ready to think many things at once.

In the classroom, despite the best of intentions, this has proven almost impossible. Graduates of what we call our "education *system*," and the academics thereof whose professional standing depends on research into what used to be called, with gross naiveté, "the facts" of literature, often make a poor audience for the poetry in poems. They want to find out what a poem means and how to use it, rather than how to follow and experience it. They have been schooled in getting to the gist of things and moving on, and so they approach poetry as if it were content covered up by words.

I take a back seat to no one in my appreciation of poetry as an occasion for conversation. But there is something overlooked in most of the conversation that surrounds poems, and that something, I have come to believe, is the poetry.

American poetry sometimes seems to be a playground of contesting ideologues, promoting themselves as narrative poets, neo-formalists, language poets, class poets, and so forth. Insofar as the techniques and manners of poetry may serve many motives, some contradictory to one another, and insofar as poetic license is not obtained from any authority other than the expressive self, I suppose that they must be, all of them, in some sense correct, no matter what they say. I think to add only this little epistemological alert: where all things are correct, it is equally true that none are.

So. Helplessness. We are, all of us, trained not to be helpless. We are schooled in what to do, as well as how, when, where, and why to do it. We become purposeful, reasonable, civic, deliberate and . . . predictable and programmable. After all that, art becomes, more and more, the refuge of our helplessness: our purposeless, unreasonable, personal or private, accidental, unpredictable selves. It is where we have a chance to experience the helpless "Yes!" of life, to experience nature and artifice, inner and outer, as if life itself were what there is to life.

As if life is what it is, nothing more. I want to be careful to respect that feeling some have, out of faith or partial research, that there is a life hereafter. Nonetheless, it seems to me that poetry springs from the need and the wish to express what this life feels like. Even when it sings of another life or another world, it sings it in the frequencies of this one.

It is good to recall, in first classes, these four lines by the Spanish poet Antonio Machado: "People possess four things/that are no good at sea:/anchor, rudder, oars, and/the fear of going down." Poetry is an abandonment of position (or anchor), an abandonment of the deliberate course (or rudder), an utter nonchalance about propulsion (or oars), and, perhaps scarily, a relinquishing of the fear of going down. Goodbye, known ports of call; goodbye, mapped interstates; goodbye, teacher with one finger held aloft; goodbye, sophisticated schooner of privilege; farewell, burden of right, the lists in the pocket.

The poet comes to his or her helplessness, and to its value, by way of the helplessness of others—and much of that masquerading as help*ful*ness. See if any of you recognize the usual poetry workshop in this description: The poet reads aloud his or her poem, hurrying through it fearfully as if it were prose garbage, and as if the greatest vulnerability is to be seen with one's mouth open. Then the discussion begins. One person says we just can't use a certain word in a

poem—it's archaic, or it's crude, or it's fancy, or—God forbid—
its meaning has to be looked up in the dictionary. Another thinks
the poem should be shorter, or longer, or should start later, or end
sooner. The group gradually cuts out all the "bad" lines, leaving, if
anything remains, a smaller poem ostensibly of "good" lines. In the
end, the group, if it is a smart one, has produced another publishable
poem in imitation of a great many other already published poems.

Little artistic growth can come from such talk. First off, one learns
nothing from others' bad work, only from one's own. Let me repeat
that because I think it may imply a way of life: one learns nothing
from others' bad work, only from one's own. Would we attempt
to learn to sing by listening to the tone deaf? Do we imagine we
could learn to fly by imitating the labors of a kangaroo? To fly, study
the eagle or the sparrow—as you prefer. To know the richness of
language, read—well, it's obvious, isn't it.

Second, the growth of a poet does not rest in what he or she can
do already. It rests in what he or she cannot do yet. In other words,
the worst part of a poem may contain the seeds of what will become
the next poem and, beyond that, bigger and better poems by that
writer.

Behind each poem brought to group discussion may lie a ghost
poem, a poem that is bigger (not necessarily longer), more complex
(not necessarily more complicated), deeper, richer, more enveloping.
To disdain the raw, unrealized portion of such a poem is to relegate
the writer to the role of good scout, on the trail of the acceptable.
I realize that one comes to a writers' conference not simply to lis-
ten, even to writers who are willing teachers, and that there is a
nurturing, supportive element to any purposeful group. Nonetheless,
the truth is that most of those whom one sees on the platforms of
writers' conferences are those of us who were too ornery to listen
to the crowd, too helpless to take good advice. We were the lucky
examples of Blake's dictum, "If the fool persist in his (or her) folly,
he (or she) shall become wise."

Ask yourself, not if you are smart enough and clever enough and
diligent enough to write the poetry to which you aspire, but if you
are dumb enough, bullish enough, helpless enough to get through.

Poems are written not from intelligence but from ignorance. The
stores are endless, the paths not yet taken innumerable. For every
real poet finds a new way with each poem by which to lose him- or

herself. One loses oneself to find oneself, if you will. One walks away from the path—the road marked by reasonable men and women who are expecting one at the other end—and creates a new path as one goes, eventually unto finding its direction, which may or may not rejoin the others where they have built what they call a civilization.

The future belongs to the helpless. I am often presented that irresistible question asked by the beginning poet: "Do you think I am any good?" I have learned to reply with a question: "If I say no, are you going to quit?" Because life offers any of us many excuses to quit. If you are going to quit now, you are almost certainly going to quit later. But I have concluded that writers are people whom you cannot stop from writing. They are helpless to stop it.

One final note about helplessness. We see now what pride and planning have brought to the so-called civilized world. The seeds of our destruction were always present in the language of our successes. The same language that enabled us to pass along the uses of fire also allows that doubletalk by which mankind creates, permits, and endorses nuclear dump sites, trickle-down economics, and the knee-jerk justifications and falsehoods of every lobby from the gun nuts to the cancer farmers. No other creature tortures; none destroys its homeland with such recklessness. Mankind is God's curse on Nature. In a world that inevitably uses language, not primarily to make art or note fact, but for lies, evasions, and distortions—all of these fed by convention and prejudice—it seems to me not only more interesting, but more useful and, yes, even virtuous—one might say, moral—for serious writing to leave at every turn the path of the willful, to fly from the calcified spine of urbanity, and to get its boots muddy.

Besides, do you really want to succeed by doing it the way you were taught? Ten years, twenty years from now, after you have published that book or books of poetry or prose, will the writing have made a difference to you? I would think it a great pleasure to be able to look in the mirror and know that you followed your instincts and that you did it your way.

Now to the issue of "fraud." I put it as I did because I was quoting a friend: Frank DiGangi, a potter. Recently, while two potters, two painters, and your humble servant were sitting around in the midst of art talk, amused by the distance between what artists know about the making of art and what the world of culture says about it, he said, "We all think we are frauds, but none of us is rich enough to say so in public." Of course, it was a joke, dependent on a sophisticated point of view and a large dose of irony. *We* are not the frauds. The frauds are those who teach art as if it were more schooling, another viewing area on the way to some invisible heaven of total under-standing where we won't have to be bothered any longer by all this confusion, this ambiguity, this ambivalence, this disorder, this, this, this . . . *life*!

Thus, in the classroom poems are presented as if they were etched in stone by writers who had, above all, A Plan. "Why does the poet say this and why does she say that?" we are asked. The better ques-tion is, "What is the *effect* of this or that?" And an even better question may be, "How do you imagine the poet happened on this or that?"

William Stafford has noted that "Writing poems is easy, like swim-ming into a fish net," but that explaining how poems are written is difficult, "like swimming out of a fish net." This is not to deny that many writers have made the act of writing sheer hell for them-selves. We have all heard how one writes by sitting in a room with a piece of paper until droplets of blood appear on one's forehead, and the one about writing being one-tenth inspiration and nine-tenths perspiration.

But it is equally true that, while ordinary trumpet players trying to play high C above the staff may turn red and threaten to go all the way to blue from the pressure, the virtuoso trumpeter Rafael Mendez could do it on a horn suspended by a string, with his hands behind his back.

I believe that for each of us there is a way of writing we can do with one hand behind our back, in a world where the telephone rings, children cry, and sometimes the doctor has bad news. If we are writers, eventually we may have the good luck to find that way. Then we will understand the true ease of the writer, that ease that seems to give him or her the powers of a medicine man or priest or psychic, and that threatens those self-proclaimed arbiters of their own tem-poral preferences, which of course they call "standards," but which time clearly shows to be nothing more than opinions.

The difficulty of writing lies in turning from our reasonable, prag-matic selves long enough to idle our way into the imagination. Once there, however, the creative engine runs smoothly and time flies past.

Poets know the experience of starting a piece just before bedtime, because one has a line or two, and then finding that it is three hours later. On the other hand, one has also labored over poems of substance that would not breathe or dance or fly, no matter how hard one worked to give them life, only to have a poem emerge suddenly all of a piece, needing little revision afterward, only a bit of correction, yet putting the other poems to shame by its richness and vitality.

About creative writing, there are some things to admit to oneself. Curmudgeons cannot admit these things, and they will not want you to admit them, either. They do not understand Kierkegaard's remark that laughter is a kind of prayer. They have no sense of humor. They do not want you to be freer than they are. They worry about what the critics of *The New Amsterdam Times* or *The New Amsterdammer* will think.

Like the members of a closed guild, they do not want the truth to be known. For the truth is that writing poetry is first a matter of getting into motion in the presence of words; that the accidental, the random, and the spontaneous are of more value to the imagination than any plan; and that it is more valuable to be able to write badly than to write well, for writing well always involves some imitation of the routine while writing badly always involves something original and raw. This is as true for formalists as for informalists and anti-formalists.

So we are all frauds, if it is fraudulent not to know what you are doing until you have done it. The truth about writing is so simple that no one can win a teaching job by admitting it. It is more and more necessary to surround such simple truths as relativity and overlap in the use of language with theories such as "structuralism" and "deconstruction." Theories are pretzel-benders. They tie us in knots.

Perhaps you have heard the saying, "He's so dumb he couldn't empty piss out of a boot if the instructions were written on the heel."

My third proposal is, "The rain is too heavy a whistle for the certainty of charity." "In actuality," like they say, that sentence is two lines of poetry I wrote more than twenty-two years ago. I knew then that they might not make a lot of sense to many readers, but to me they contained the essence of naturalism, metaphysics, and morality—and, thus, poetry. While I went on writing what I could, these lines stayed with me, suggesting a kind of poem I was not yet prepared to write.

In the beginning, I had tried to go forward from those two lines, in this way:

> The rain
> is too heavy a whistle for the certainty of charity.
> The moon
> throws us off the sense.
> The wind
> happens at night before you drop off.
> The mountains
> on them sufferance blisters its skin of paint.
> The oceans
> in which this happens.
> The ash
> of which we are made.

Later, I used some of the lines in a poem about a home-sewn pillow. The pillow, which supported me for years, is finally shedding its cover and spilling its guts, while these twelve lines of poetry remain pristine and withholding.

But not unapproachable. For while I have not yet written the rest of the poem, I feel that I am now closer to it. I understand now—no, I *feel* now—its mix of external and internal, of reaching and reticence. If I have had anything on my mind over the years of writing, beyond each single poem as it came into being, if I have hoped for more than a momentary illumination, it has been for this. So much comes to mind in relation to that ideal that I cannot tell you all of it. On the low side of specificity, there are the many other examples I have found and cared for: this one, for example, by Theodore Roethke, the start of an elegy: "Is that dance slowing in the mind of man/ That made him think the universe could hum?" And on the high side of the general, there is Pound's quotation from, he says, De Quincey or Coleridge (he is not himself sure which) to the effect that, "The character of a great poet is everywhere present yet nowhere visible as a distinct excitement."

And where did I find, other than in living day to day, the sense of the complex that made such sense to me? I found it in poems other people did not care about, in the raw language of journals and letters, and in poetry in translation.

More and more I want my poetry raw or abstract. In the words of an old song, I "don't want to mess with Mr. In Between."

Listen to this report by a therapist, written after a session with someone called "Robin":

I used to call him The Hound of Hell, that's how bad he was. Now he talks. He says, "When I walk into that house it's like the air has fists." A mean place he's from. I may be the first who ever held his tears. "I've been reading Gertrude Stein in the way that you instructed me, just listening to the sounds," he said, and once he said the word *henceforth*. Nearly fell off my rocker that day. He wrote me a letter, he wrote, "Amazing how quickly snow disappears." He wrote he would like to be an athlete or Thomas Mann, he loves that guy. He wrote he thinks I would like his dog better than him. He brought in a book about a boy who thought spiders had ears in their legs which he wanted to discuss instead of his father who shouted Shut Up before he even opened his mouth. "How does poetry enter the mind," he asks. "Gee, and then sometimes it just packs up and leaves." People grow to love what is repeated, who said that? Today before he goes he makes a kiss and bats it to me, then says, "Dead writers are best. They stay the same so long."

Or how about this helpless, shockingly innocent journal entry from a junior at a high school in Georgia:

Yesterday I messed around with everything and goofed off all day. I gave away five of my bulldog pups yesterday. Eddie Burgess got three and Lynn Beck and Romeo got two. I went over to Ma's about dark and ate supper. Then I went home.

I have been writing about my life and I have realized that you don't understand some things. I will explain. I live by myself. I live about a mile and a half from my ma. I used to be married. I was married to Terri Metts. She was five months pregnant. I had a 1966 Chevy Chevelle it had a nice white paint job and rally wheels. It had a 350 4-bolt mane with a four-speed transmission and a 4:11 rear end. Terri never drove it. I let her drive it one day to the Handy Corner in Dawson County. On the way back she wrecked. She lost the baby. She was in the Hospital three months and I never went to see her. I loved my car. She died. I now have a 69 roadrunner it is black and gold with a 440 plus 6 and a 4 speed and high speed rear end, a 77 Ford ranger, 351 Cleveland and 3 speed on column with a spicer rear end. It is painted black. I also have two motorcycles a Yamaha maxim and Yamaha 360. I dig graves for a living that is how I afford my vehicles.

By the way, I was deliberately exaggerating when I said a moment ago that I wanted my poetry, if not raw, to be abstract. Truly, what attracts me in poetry other than the raw is not abstraction itself, but the quality of abstraction that comes out of the generalized. And what connects the generalized to the abstract is metaphor, with its peculiar ability to contain a thing without it being the thing itself.

Remember, if you will, that, while modern poetry may begin somewhere back in, say, Baudelaire, where the image became the repository for a mixture of the objective and the subjective all at once (that mix came to be the essence of modernism, even a formula for it), something else we might as well call "contemporary poetry" begins in a subsequent awareness of the general condition of man and the universe. Some people might say it begins with "The Bomb," but The Bomb of the fifties was only a localized blot on the Malthusian landscape. After that, we came to know much more.

Some artists brag about not watching television, not reading newspapers, and the like. One understands their brand of escapism. Some people can sense a totality in private. I will say, however, that I think generalized knowledge, rather than the particularity of book learning—what used to be called wisdom as distinct from intelligence—is one of the signs of contemporary art.

So. I come back to the water and the singing string of charity. I feel with a strength I have not felt earlier the rightness of any line two. When the Exxon Valdez layered Prince William Sound with oil, the story floated all the way down to the Lower Forty-eight. And there on a day when we fed the marmot, and then the deer, breaking the rules, with a study of pulp mills just about to be released in a new report on cancer, and Chinese armor poised to roll over the student rebellion, and everywhere in the world something else, the DiGangis were celebrating their thirtieth wedding anniversary all year long, so that, feeling the impulse to dance as much as to run, we all knew that, when we talk about poetry, we are talking about a perfect vacancy, resonant and responsive to whomever takes up residence and stays.

Stay up half the night for a week and write one hundred poems. Write badly, rawly, smoothly, accidentally, irrationally. . . . Join the disparate. Make the "like" unlike and the "unlike" like. When you can't write, read. Use the word "window" in every line. Write about colors. Set out to write a poem "like a sweater." It makes no difference. The coherence is already within you. Afterwards, you will have learned more about writing than an entire semester of classes can teach you.

In writing, as in the imagination, as in dreams, there is no right way, and there is no one way. Thus, one does not require a compass, just a good supply of nourishment and a push.

At this point, I am going to interrupt the main thrust of my paper, which has four paragraphs to go, to strengthen or weaken my case with a bit more testimony. Those four paragraphs yet to come, when I reach them, will explain my title and otherwise conclude my presentation.

First, I would like to try to illustrate some implications of believing that there is no one way and no right way. The poem I am putting before us is not put here for praise but for attention. The illustration and testimony I offer is that of a common reader.

*Lawn Sprawled Out Like a Dog*

When the peacock screams out at night, do you think it knows
its cry makes a man look at himself to see if he is suffering?
Perhaps the peacock and all birds realize
the effect of their voices. They carry a musical score in their bones,

which are so thin—toothpicks, really—their only defenses
are the gluttony that puffs them up, the edges of their songs and cries,
and the flimsy handkerchiefs on struts
they wave as they fly or run from grass to grass.

Even the tiny mosquito, most blood-thirsty of God's creations,
considering the brevity of its life, must sense the communion to come
when, shivering and wild,
with nothing to eat, she sings us to the wood like Circe.

Forgive me, I mixed up the horrible little mosquito, an insect,
with the eagle, the loon and the brave, little sparrow.
Forgive me, I only recently learned
to slap down the gnats that hover near the shores of human swans!

In the reading of poetry, it sometimes seems that one encounters example after example of willful misunderstanding. I would like to propose an opposing attitude: that of willful *un*derstanding. From such small acts of sympathy, great rewards may follow.

Hence, lacking any attribution to the contrary, one could perhaps imagine this poem to have been written in a language other than English and then translated. I rather like that quality myself. Perhaps Spanish, given the surreal quality of the title and last line. Or

Russian—Russian writers, we believe, are free with sentiment and such words as "suffering." Or perhaps the poem was translated from one of the languages of Eastern Europe, given the satiric bent of the last two lines, a turn on social expectation and civilized blindness. It could even be British, if I hear the tone of voice correctly in the phrase "toothpicks, really" and sense the exacting attitude that turns bird wings into flimsy handkerchiefs.

All of this interests me. As does the bizarre sympathy in stanza three of the speaker for the mosquito. Who among us has considered a blood bank for mosquitos?

Who is being addressed? We don't know. *I* don't know. Could be it's the reader who is asked to imagine the knowledge, or awareness, possessed by other animals. Easy to do, or at least to think about, perhaps, when it's the peacock crying out in the dark with its all-too-human voice. Easy to move from there to bird song at large. There is much less to a bird than we are led to believe by our wishes, our fancy, and its own skillful song. But even if we are made to concentrate, still the eagle is noble; the loon, elegant and mysterious; and the common sparrow, brave beyond number. But the mosquito?

I lean forward as a reader when I come upon, first, a title so imbued—for me, that is—imbued with a suddenness of imagination encircling ordinary things, and, second, an initial sentence that mixes location and involvement and raises the stakes in a hurry. In leaning into the poem, I get caught up by what might be called a "narrative of mind." In this case, the poem plays off the self-serving distinctions we make between ourselves and other sentient beings. This is the sort of theme that engages me when it is left to simmer underneath everything else, because I don't believe in crystal power, I don't think aliens are coming to save us, channelers are frauds, a sucker is born every minute and the truth will set you free.

In the end, I have to go back to the title, the strangest phrase in the poem. I can make more sense of it than I could before I read the lines that follow it. I see that it combines distance (I hear the echo of the phrase "a sprawling lawn") and locus (I see a sprawled out dog). I see, when I linger on it, that the image is an amalgamation of nature and animal, and that it now parallels the last image in the poem in which animal and human are likewise combined in "the necks of human swans." Of course, swans are swans and humans are humans. Aren't they?

I do not think this poem shies from its human role, nor refuses its guilty survival. I do see that it questions conventional distinctions within a somewhat bizarre frame, and that it handles notions of suffering and survival.

I like this poem because of its "Russian" sentimentality, its "Spanish" imagery, its "East European" irony, its "British" nuances, its strangeness, the elasticity of its line, and other things as well. I like it because I have paid enough attention to it as a reader to have been rewarded. And of course I like it because—and I recommend this reason to all of you—I like it because, yes, because I wrote it. However, I am not employing it here today because of who wrote it, but because of how it was written.

"In actual fact," like they say, I wrote it during a gathering in Fairbanks, Alaska, as part of a week's testimonial. I wanted to show my students that I meant it when I recommended that they write more, starting with whatever was at hand and daring to be odd. And so I wrote a poem a day. And at the end included them in a public reading. This is the one I kept. The title is a line reported as having come up in another class which was looking for a starting point for an assignment. It had been mentioned during a panel discussion at the start of the week. Later I realized that, because the line is unconventional, unsocialized, it required of me a human definition. And the human definition, in turn, led me into a brief meditation on the human condition. And so it goes.

As I approach the end of my talk, I want to refer back to the moment when I realized that it had to have a title. It is sometimes bad to write with a title in mind. With a title in mind, that practical fellow or gal each of us can be sticks to the subject. If I had one minute to tell you a single piece of advice for writing poetry, and if I wanted to be certain your poetry would surprise you and others, and if above all I hoped your poetry would not be simply that kind of writing which goes gently to its end in the interest of soporific culture—if I had but one minute to say one thing, I would say, Don't stick to the subject. (The second thing I would say is, Listen!)

Afterwards—the title comes afterwards. Well, I had three items in mind at the beginning, so "Three Propositions" seemed seductively syllogistic. But those kinds of propositions are not so much fun, so I added three names: Hooey, Dewey, and Loony. If this seems silly, may I remind you that T. S. Eliot and Groucho Marx entered into a correspondence, including an exchange of photographs of themselves, and that, when Marx at last went to dinner at the Eliots, brushing up on "Macbeth" so that he might have the intellectual nourishment he craved, Eliot wanted only to talk about "Duck Soup."

"Hooey," because most of what is said about writing poetry, after the event—often by critics, reviewers and theorists, but sometimes by the poets themselves—is just that: hooooeeee! "Dewey," because as a schoolboy I had a fond spot for the so-called practical philosopher, John Dewey, who among other things suggested that classroom chairs should not be bolted down. And "Loony," because after all, by any reasonable standard of society at large, anyone who writes what some of us have written, or—heaven forfend—suggests that there might be utter clarity in the lines "The rain/is too heavy a whistle for the certainty of charity" must certainly be loony.

So let us go then, you and I, when the evening is spread out against the sky like a pigeon poised upon a nickel. Let us not get into a pickle. Or, finding ourselves already deep in the briny pickley flesh, let us find there the seeds of our poetry. What rough beast, its hour come round at last, slouches toward Bethlehem to be born? No one knows. Is this a dish for fat lips? Roethke wasn't sure. Is that dance slowing in the mind of man that made him think the universe could hum? Yes, it is.

# Bloody Brain Work

W R I T I N G  poetry is a way of life, not a career.

\* \* \*

Ray Mullen, potter and painter, on his retirement from teaching: "No matter what you make, you can't buy a day of your life."

\* \* \*

Word comes from eastern Long Island that another of my favorite former teachers has died.

\* \* \*

Mike, and Mike's brother, Perry, whose card identifies him as "the P-Man," have come to haul away some bedsprings, the heavy bank teller's machine that Jason and friends pushed up the driveway into the carport a decade ago, and some metal storage shelves from Sears that were our first bookcases. Perry spots my wooden wagon and wants to buy it to fix it up. The sides are missing, but okay. Dorothy tells him the story of how I got the wagon, how I fell as a small child and split open my head and had to go to the doctor for stitches and how after that I wouldn't get a haircut because all I knew is that someone in a white coat wanted to do something to my head. So my father gave Johnny-the-Barber a red wagon with which to tempt me on my way home from school. Dorothy tells Perry the story in the hope that the story will go with the wagon, and of course she's right: material things are not a life but evidence of a life.

\* \* \*

And Mike's brother says, "Every kid ought to have a wagon that has a story attached to it. When I was a kid, I had a disease that was dissolving my hip joint. I had to be in a body cast for thirteen months. So my father bought me a little metal wagon and my sister used to pull me around the trailer park. One day we got too wild and I fell out and broke the body cast, so they had to take me back to the hospital and I had to have it done all over again."

\* \* \*

Mike will have to come back to take away my radio equipment, from the days when I was W2IDK. Amateur radio was a way of life, not a career. This was before transistors replaced tubes and technology made single sideband sound normal. Before that, a voice on single sideband (which takes half as much room on the dial as a normal modulated voice signal) sounded like Donald Duck. On Field Day, we'd put up tents, string antennas and mount beams, fix up places to sleep and to cook, start up the generators and stay on the air for two days to test our ability in emergencies. "Hams" were strange people then, oddballs who knew something and who shared their information generously but who didn't care if others heard about them or not. The "shack" (an attic) where I first heard the mysteries of short wave and code belonged to W2EBT. "Two Eggs, Bacon & Toast," he called himself, and "Elderly, Bald & Toothless." The shack in the woods where I built my first transmitter, a twenty-watt piezoelectric crystal-controlled oscillator, and power supply, belonged to the reclusive W2OQI ("Two Ossified Queer Indians"), who showed me how, and I caught a ride to radio club meetings with W2FCH (Herbert Snell, who called himself "Two Females Chasing Herbie").

\* \* \*

Now I sometimes wander out to the cliffs at Fort Worden, outside Port Townsend, Washington, where in June the local hams still set up for Field Day. But now they use tv and fax machines, their transmitters are tiny, their beam antennas don't have to go up on trees to fall over, and they eat and sleep in campers and trailers. When Mike wants to, he can take away my Lysco 600-watt transmitter, my HQ129X receiver, which came from the radio room of a Coast Guard boat, my Vibroflex key with its repeating dot key, and the rest of it. I see the c.w. operators at Field Day using their monokeys, which have repeating dot and dash keys both, with the result that their "fists" have no personalities. I learned plenty from my time as a ham radio operator, but I'm glad I didn't stay to be overcome by technical gee-whiz and the comforts of home.

\* \* \*

And Mike can take away my photo enlarger and the rest of the darkroom equipment. Those were great days, the days of Aaron Siskind and Harry Callahan and Ansel Adams and Robert Heinecken and Nathan Lyons and Walter Chappell and Henry Holmes Smith and Van Deren Coke and the young Jerry Uelsmann and Clarence John Laughlin and Art Sinsabaugh and Minor White and a whole generation of hot young photographers gathered around Minor at the Rochester Institute of Technology and around Siskind and Callahan at the Institute of Design in Chicago. I met some of these photographers while attending Alfred University, and others when I lived in Syracuse and Rochester and still others when I lived in Chicago. This, too, was a community, and creative photography was a way of life, not a career. Nowadays photography is taught in most art departments. For a while, even after I stopped photographing, I'd be asked to visit photography classes. But the students wanted to talk about photography, while I thought we should talk about pictures, and then when they put up their pictures most of the things they hung were related to photographs as rendering is to drawing. These weren't art, they were technique. These weren't compositions, they were symbolic records. The students would resist whenever I suggested they put aside their 35-mm direct viewfinder cameras and start using cameras with ground glass viewfinders so that they could learn about light and composition. They took photographs that were literary illustrations. They were earnest students on a career track, and they didn't, wouldn't, and couldn't understand. There continued to be many good photographer-artists at work in this country, but their images soon floated in a sea of images while viewers paused only for the sensationalistic.

\* \* \*

As for my own photos, I let them go to seed. I was all set to print a portfolio of nudes—pieces of the body sculpted by light—for Margaret Randall's bilingual magazine out of Mexico, *El Corno Emplumado*, when I stopped photographing and printing. I had learned to see as a photographer, which was of more moment to me than producing pictures to frame. It was a way of life, not a career. All that remains on our walls from that time are three images I made without the camera by printing paper "negatives" torn from the funnies: both sides of the page can be seen along with the dots (holes) in the screens then used to print newspaper graphics.

\* \* \*

I haven't yet decided if I'm going to give away my cornet and trumpet. The cornet is a Bach handmade job, built before the Bach factory sold out to Conn, a horn that used to belong to Ned Mahoney, who sat second chair to James Burke, the virtuoso soloist with the Edwin Franko Goldman Band. Many a time my friend Roger and I sat in the front row at the Goldman Band concerts in New York City's Central Park with the score to that night's solo spread out on our laps. And the trumpet is an Olds Mendez with two triggers (to flatten the normally sharp tones when the first or third valves are pressed, though one can do this by lip). I used that horn to play Jeremiah Clarke's "Trumpet Voluntary" with Dan Clayton in black robes from the pulpit on Easter. Music was my introduction to artists and nighthawks. I don't think I have ever lost the feeling that late hours and creative expression go together. (I began this essay after midnight. It is now 3:30 A.M. What time will I quit to sleep?—About 6 A.M.) We horn players were a community. We tried to make money, but there wasn't much to be made, so it had to be a way of life for most of us, not a career. Yes, my music teacher hoped I'd go to music school, but the idea was to become a teacher. The idea then was always first to earn a living and then to take private time for art.

\* \* \*

I've seen Carl Fracassini recently, in New Mexico where he is retired. Frac was my pottery and drawing teacher, and he doesn't expect to live much longer. He asked me to pick some of his drawings to take home. He was a great teacher and a wonderful artist who lacked the pretensions of his colleagues—he preferred to cook and build and hunt and fish and make pots and drawings and create a community among his students—and so he never received the full measure of respect he deserved at the university. No matter to those of us who learned quality and community from him. Mike won't have to take away any pots. Except for a couple that Dorothy rescued, I broke them all when I gave up potting.

\* \* \*

I visit a sophomore "core literature" class to observe one of my advisees. The teacher does her job well, and the class is alert, but these are students from "ordinary" backgrounds like mine—not the children of professionals but of workers and small business owners, probably raised largely without the benefits of special classes, private schools, foreign travel, or substantial home libraries. They lack the courage to be articulate, so they speak in an all-purpose colloquial flow designed to show how well they fit in rather than how they stand out: plenty of "you know's" and "I mean's" and "kind of's," lots of "like's" but no "as if's," all of their speech having a general quality of imprecision that nonetheless communicates what they wish to express so long as things remain simple. They seem to understand what they mean, but they never quite say it. Ultimately, as with imprecision in poetry, when the conversation grows more complex, they will be able to say neither what they understand nor what they do not understand. Most of the time, however, it won't make any difference.

\* \* \*

In the poetry seminar, we have been reading Bishop and O'Hara, with Dugan and Jarrell on tap. Bishop comes up first. What a pleasure to read poetry bearing such precise powers of observation, such precision of language, and such careful and effective rhetorical emphasis, with the courage of open-faced and even-handed syntax, the courage of accessibility, the courage not to overwrite, the courage to have a viewpoint without faking a vision. The whole group feels it. This is one of those seminars in which, if the members of the class want to absorb new influences, I'm game. Bell's rules: (1) No one has to write a "good" poem; and (2) teacher has to do the assignment too. The first time, we write poems after the fashion of Bishop or O'Hara. In fact, we write our own poems but under the flag of surrender to some aspect of another's poem. In a later meeting, I hand out a few poems by Neruda from an early book, *Residence on Earth*. Let's see if we can combine Bishop's reticence and observation with Neruda's abandon, Bishop's vertical thrust with Neruda's horizontal speed. What I don't say is that it doesn't matter whether or not they can actually do it, but only that the assigned influences and the deadline take them away from any self-absorption or self-importance, including *a priori* themes and agendas. Also, that they give themselves permission to fail. And that they learn, eventually, the value of the arbitrary when it receives sufficient attention—but that is more complicated than needs be said.

\* \* \*

A little Neruda goes a long way. I make a crack to the effect that our lives are filled with passion and physical detail, while in American poetry hysteria and anxiety often pass for passion, and filler takes the place of observation. I think to myself, but don't say aloud, that we have a band of poetry critics whose own prose styles naturally lead them to prefer overwriting of all kinds, which they may perhaps think is a signal of literary ambition.

\* \* \*

During the core literature class, I wrote down, "Literature is for beginners." I was thinking about thinking. Because, for the poet, after all, poetry is the result, not the intention. Poetry is the residue of bloody brain work, the signal that a process has taken place that fosters an emotional approach to thinking. All technique is subsumed in what we later call the "poetic" quality of the text. All the fame in the world is secondary to the epiphanic moment when the poem began to cohere. For the poet, the true consequence is the next poem: hence, a way of life, not a career.

\* \* \*

Deby Groover, a potter and printmaker from Athens, Georgia, tells me over coffee that her first pottery teacher said to the class, "If you have any attachment to anything you make, then you better go ahead and break it now."

\* \* \*

I don't have any heavy poetry equipment for Mike to haul away. I do plan to sell my papers and many of my books soon. I need to clear some space. Poetry has accumulated around me. I didn't set out to teach where I teach. I set out to earn a living, figuring I could write no matter what. I had a wonderful son at an early age and, when the marriage ended, I kept him with me. I had to make a living. I wouldn't have had it any other way. Still, when I was asked to return to the Writers' Workshop, I hesitated before saying yes. It was still a community then, a smaller community, finding its direction inside the community. Today, like other writing programs, it's heavy on visitors and events, with a decided emphasis on official reputations, and it thus takes its instructions from outside. Like other universities, mine now constantly measures its standing and judges its faculty in ways that damage the community. In this dog-eat-dog economy, education, too, has become more of a career than a way of life.

\* \* \*

My seminar students had dropped off but one poem to be xeroxed for class. I had mine: that made two. I was downhearted: hadn't they been able to become selfless enough, to improvise, to swing, to play, to relax, to get down, couldn't those who were wearing the emperor's new clothing shed it to believe in the referential possibilities of words, hadn't they seen the lesson of Bishop's poems and O'Hara's and Neruda's, absent the fawning criticism and the literary fighting for position that follows them, hadn't they understood that those three poets were finally just like them?

\* \* \*

And then they came to class, which is held at our home, and Dorothy put out things to eat and drink, and we let some Tom Waits play as we gathered, and they had all written their poems after all and xeroxed them in time, and the freshness of their words and the emotional weight of their pretend-abandon made our group of poems written to deadline a better worksheet than they could expect in any of the sections of the graduate poetry workshop where their more "important" and "original" poems were to be discussed—the ones they made up from ambition and order and fancy talk—and some of them were saying that they were planning to put these poems on the worksheets for the other classes, and we said okay, next week it's all O'Hara and the week after that it will be all Bishop and then it will be Dugan, and once again the world was all right if it could provide this sort of opportunity for community and thought and high spirits with writing at the core.

\* \* \*

Poetry is a way of life, not a career. A career means you solicit the powerful and the famous. A way of life means you live where you are with the people around you. A career means you become an authority. A way of life means you stay a student, even if you teach for a living. A career means your life increasingly comes from your art. A way of life means your art continues to arise from your life. Careerism feeds on the theoretical, the fancified, the complicated, the coded, and the overwrought: all forms of psychological cowardice. A way of life is nourished by the practical, the unadorned, the complex, and a direct approach to the mysterious. Obscurity is a celebrated path to nowhere, an affliction. For poetry to be a way of life in a referential world, it requires of us the courage of clarity—linear, syntactical, and referential—which in no way compromises the great wildness of experience and imagination (think of Bishop, O'Hara, Neruda, Dugan, Jarrell . . . ). The rewards for this courage and this surrender to influence (a form of community) and clarity are beyond career.

\* \* \*

Which are you pursuing: a way of life or a career? The scent of literary careerism has never been stronger. Conversely, the need for each of us to find a way of life—to quote a Dugan poem, "personal life wrung from mass issues in a bloody time and lived out hiddenly"—has never been of more moment.

\* \* \*

To most of my current and past students, thank you, wherever you are. To W2EBT and W2OQI and W2FCH, to my dead teachers and friends, to the last few who remember how it was in the arts, to those who still practice in secret or solitude, to Robert Heinecken on his impending retirement, to the sound of Miles Davis playing standards through a straight mute, to all those in my life with pizazz and humility whose lingo had the snap of reality and the metabolic shiver of deep feeling and who did not judge and compete but laughed a lot—my mortal indebtedness.

# A DEAD MAN SAMPLER

# Preface to *The Book of the Dead Man*

B E F O R E  the Dead Man, minus-1 was still an imaginary number.

The Dead Man will have nothing more to do with the conventional Ars Poetica, that blind manifesto allegiant to the past. Let the disenchanted loyalist reconsider the process. Among motives, occasions, codes, needs and knuckle-head accidents, the Dead Man accepts all and everything. He knows in his bones that writing is metabolic.

What are we to make of the Dead Man's reference to Keats? That poetry should come, as Keats wrote, "as naturally as the Leaves to a tree"? To this the Dead Man has added the dimension of the minus. He understands that fallibility and ignorance are the true stores, the bottomless reservoirs of creation. He is the fount *for* that spillover. As for the tedium of objects distorted from their long imprisonment in books, the Dead Man has learned that to be satiated is not to be satisfied.

So he furthers the love affair between the sentence and the line. Whereas formerly the line took a missionary position, under the rule of the Dead Man the sentence once more invigorates the line. The ongoing attempt by dictionary makers to define "poetry," as it has been called, is an object of derision to the Dead Man. The Dead Man knows that every technique is passé except when reencountered at its birth. The Dead Man moves as comfortably among nightingales as among house wrens.

"Perfected fallibility": that's the key, the solace, the right number (one of one, two of two, three of three, etc.). Hence, the fragment is more than the whole. The Dead Man is a material mystic. His hourglass is bottomless. No. 27 ("About the Dead Man and *The Book of the Dead Man*") reminds us that the Dead Man is "a postscript

223

to closure," and "the resident tautologist in an oval universe that is robin's-egg-blue to future generations."

Has it not already been stated of the Dead Man in the poem "About the Dead Man and His Poetry" that he is the tautologist, the postscript, perfected fallibility, etc.? Yes. The Dead Man tells the truth the first time. The Dead Man, too, writes as he has to— with a watch cap and a sweatshirt, with a leaking skull and dilapidated lungs, at an hour beyond clocks. He lives on hunger. He eats his words.

Before the birth of the Dead Man, it was not possible to return. It was not possible, it was pre-conceptual, it was discretionary to the point of chaos and accident to return, since of course there was nowhere yet to return to. Since the birth of the Dead Man, however, it is possible, even likely, that one may return. From the future, one walks ever more slowly into the past.

All this the Dead Man knows. As for me, I know nothing. But do not think one can know nothing so easily. It has taken me many years.

M. B.

# The Book of the Dead Man (#3)

## 1. About the Beginnings of the Dead Man

When the dead man throws up, he thinks he sees his inner life.

Seeing his vomit, he thinks he sees his inner life.

Now he can pick himself apart, weigh the ingredients, research his makeup.

He wants to study things outside himself if he can find them.

Moving, the dead man makes the sound of bone on bone.

He bends a knee that doesn't wish to bend, he raises an arm that argues with a shoulder, he turns his head by throwing it wildly to the side.

He envies the lobster the protective sleeves of its limbs.

He believes the jellyfish has it easy, floating, letting everything pass through it.

He would like to be a starfish, admired for its shape long after.

Everything the dead man said, he now takes back.

Not as a lively young man demonstrates sincerity or regret.

A young dead man and an old dead man are two different things.

A young dead man is oil, an old dead man is water.

A young dead man is bread and butter, an old dead man is bread and water—it's a difference in construction, also architecture.

The dead man was there in the beginning: to the dead man, the sky is a crucible.

In the dead man's lifetime, the planet has changed from lava to ash to cement.

But the dead man flops his feathers, he brings his wings up over his head and has them touch, he bends over with his beak to the floor, he folds and unfolds at the line where his armor creases.

The dead man is open to change and has deep pockets.

The dead man is the only one who will live forever.

## 2. More About the Beginnings of the Dead Man

One day the dead man looked up into the crucible and saw the sun.
The dead man in those days held the sky like a small globe, like a
    patchwork ball, like an ultramarine bowl.
The dead man softened it, kneaded it, turned it and gave it volume.
He thrust a hand deep into it and shaped it from the inside out.
He blew into it and pulled it and stretched it until it became
    full-sized, a work of art created by a dead man.
The excellence of it, the quality, its character, its fundamental
    nature, its *raison d'être*, its "it" were all indebted to the
    dead man.

The dead man is the flywheel of the spinning planet.
The dead man thinks he can keep things the same by not moving.
By not moving, the dead man maintains the status quo at the center
    of change.
The dead man, by not moving, is an explorer: he follows his nose.
When it's not personal, not profound, he can make a new world
    anytime.
The dead man is the future, was always the future, can never be
    the past.
Like God, the dead man existed before the beginning, a time
    marked by galactic static.
Now nothing remains of the first static that isn't music, fashioned
    into melody by the accidents of interval.
Now nothing more remains of silence that isn't sound.
The dead man has both feet in the past and his head in the clouds.

# The Book of the Dead Man (#14)

## 1. About the Dead Man and Government

Under Communism, the dead man's poems were passed around
hand-to-hand.

The dead man's poems were dog-eared, positively, under
Communism.

The dead man remembers Stalin finally strangling on verbs.

And the dead man's poems were mildewed from being hidden in
basements under Fascism.

Embedded in the dead man is a picture of Mussolini hanging from
a noun.

The dead man didn't know what to say first, after the oppression
was lifted.

The green cast of mildew gave way to the brown stain of coffee
upon coffee.

Suddenly, a pen was a pen and an alligator only an alligator.

A pig in boots was no longer a human being, a dead man was no
longer alive though everyone knew better.

Now the dead man feels the steamy weight of the world.

He trembles at the press of the witch hunters, their clothes
like night.

He has in his memory all tortures, genocides, trials and lockups.

He sees the lovers of pressed flowers brought down by botanical
poverty.

He sees the moviegoers, who kissed through the credits, stunned by
the sudden light after the ending.

In the lobby, the dead man's manuscripts went under coats and into
pockets.

Then they all went off to spill coffee and argue ethics.

The dead man is the anarchist whose eyes look up through the
bottom of the glass raised in toast.

The dead man is sweeter than life. Sweeter than life is the life of the
dead man.

## 2. *More About the Dead Man and Government*

The dead man votes once for Abraham Lincoln, but that's it.

That's all he's time for (one man/one vote), so the dead man votes for Abe Lincoln.

The dead man votes with his feet, lashing his possessions to his back as if he were Ulysses tied to the mast to resist the siren call to stay put.

The dead man votes with a gun, disassembling it, beating the parts into scrap metal for farm implements.

The dead man votes with wet hands, a fishy smell lemon juice can't cut.

He comes in off the boat, off the farm, from the cash register and the time clock to throw down a ballot.

The dead man is there when the revolution stalls in a pile of young corpses.

It is the dead man's doing when the final tally is zero to zero.

The dead man is the freight man on the swing shift at the end of the line.

The dead man remembers the railroads run down by automobiles, the fields commandeered for storm sewers, the neighborhoods knifed by highways.

The dead man thinks a dead Lincoln is still better than the other candidates.

He knows that death stops nothing, and he hopes to be placed among the censored.

His immortality depends on the quality of his enemies.

He sees a wormy democracy spilling from the graveyards, its fists flailing at the target.

There is hope, there is still hope, there is always hope.

The dead man and his fellow dead are the buried treasure which will ransom the future.

You have only to believe in the past.

# The Book of the Dead Man (#23)

## 1. About the Dead Man and His Masks

When the dead man thinks himself exposed, he puts on a mask.

Thinking himself exposed, the dead man puts on a mask.

Before he needed a mask, he wore his medals on his chest and his heart on his sleeve.

The dead man wears the mask of tomfoolery, the mask of assimilation, the mask of erasure, the scarred mask, the teen mask, the mask with the built-in *oh*, the laughing mask, the crying mask, the secretive mask, the telltale mask, and of course the death mask.

The dead man's masks are as multifarious as the wiles of a spider left to work in the bushes.

To the dead man, a spider's web is also a mask, and he wears it.

The trail of a slug is a mask, and the vapors from underground fires are a mask, and the dead light of sunset is a mask, and the dead man wears each of them.

The dead man curtained off the world, now everything between them is a mask.

He weaves masks of sand and smoke, of refracted light and empty water.

The dead man takes what the world discards: hair and bones, urine and blood, ashes and sewage.

The dead man, reconstituted, will not stay buried, reappearing in disguises that fool no one yet cast doubt.

He comes to the party wearing the face of this one or that one, scattering the shadows as he enters.

When there is no one face, no two faces, no fragility of disposition, no anticipation, no revelation at midnight, then naturally years pass without anyone guessing the identity of the dead man.

It is no longer known if the dead man was at the funeral.

## 2. More About the Dead Man and His Masks

The dead man's mask prefigures all *ism*'s such as surrealism,
    patriotism, cronyism, futurism, Darwinism, barbarism,
    dadaism, Catholicism, Judaism, etc.
Many of the dead man's masks are museum pieces: final
    expressions from Death Row, those startled at the last second in
    Pompeii or Dresden or Hiroshima, faces surprised in the
    trenches, the terror of furnaces and lime, a look formed from
    suffocation or lengthy bleeding or embalming.
The dead man apologizes for leaving a sewing machine and an
    umbrella on the operating table.
The dead man catalogs war memorials, potter's fields, he takes
    stock of undiscovered suicides, pseudonyms and all instances of
    anonymity.
The dead man's masks are composed of incongruous materials
    accidentally combined and are as rare and wild as certain edible
    fungi that closely resemble poisonous mushrooms.
He doffs his hat to long hair, moustaches and beards, but does not
    give himself away.
He greets the grieving, the relieved, the startled, the victimized and
    the triumphant without letting on.
The dead man's hands are twice as expressive in gloves, his feet
    deprived of their arches gain momentum in shoes, and his mask
    shields him from those who wish to trade knowledge for truth.
The dead man's first mask was a hand over his mouth.

# Acknowledgments

My grateful acknowledgments to the editors of the publications in which these heretofore uncollected pieces appeared previously:

"Cryptic Version of Ecstasy," *The Gettysburg Review*.
"Eastern Long Island," *Poems for a Small Planet: Contemporary Nature Poetry*, Middlebury College Press/University Press of New England, 1993.
"Ecstasy," *The Gettysburg Review*.
"Ending with a Line from Lear," *The Atlantic* and *Contemporary Authors Autobiography Series*, Gale Research, 1991.
"Just a Moment—I Am Busy Being a Man," *The Virginia Quarterly Review*.
"March," *Stand* (England).
"Poem in Orange Tones," *The Georgia Review*.
"Pulsations," *Poems for a Small Planet: Contemporary Nature Poetry*, 1993.
"Short Version of Ecstasy," *Orbis* (England).
"The Hen," *The Atlantic*.
"The Uniform," *Stand*.
"We Tried to Stop the War," *Sarajevo: An Anthology for Bosnian Relief*, Elgin Community College (Illinois).

"Pages" (Series #1), *The Antioch Review*.
"Pages" (Series #2), *The American Poetry Review*.
"Pages" (Series #3): the poem dated 8/2/87 and the paragraph titled "Meditation on Kicking Over the Traces" appeared in *Ploughshares*.

"What Became What: An Autobiography," *Contemporary Authors Autobiography Series*, Gale Research, 1991.

"Bloody Brain Work," *The American Poetry Review* and *The Pushcart Prize*, vol. XVIII, 1993.

"The 'Technique' of Rereading," *New England Review*; *Poetics: Essays on the Art of Poetry*, Tendril, 1984; and *Conversant Essays: Contemporary Poets on Poetry*, Wayne State University Press, 1990.

"Three Propositions: Hooey, Dewey, and Loony," *The American Poetry Review*; *Writers on Writing*, Middlebury College Press/University Press of New England, 1991; and *The Pushcart Prize*, vol. XVI, 1991.

Previously collected poems appeared in the following books: *Things We Dreamt We Died For* (Stone Wall Press, 1966); *A Probable Volume of Dreams* (Atheneum, 1969); *Residue of Song* (Atheneum, 1974); *Stars Which See, Stars Which Do Not See* (Atheneum, 1977); *These Green-Going-to-Yellow* (Atheneum, 1981); *Drawn by Stones, by Earth, by Things That Have Been in the Fire* (Atheneum, 1984); and *New and Selected Poems* (Atheneum, 1987).

"The Hours Musicians Keep," "Entry for *The Poets' Encyclopedia*: Five-and-Ten," and "Noun/Object/Image" appeared in *Old Snow Just Melting: Essays and Interviews* (University of Michigan Press, 1983).

Thanks, also, to Sam Hamill and Tree Swenson of Copper Canyon Press for permission to reprint the following from books in print:

From *Iris of Creation*: "A Man May Change," "A Primer about the Flag," "He Had a Good Year," "How He Grew Up," "Lawn Sprawled Out Like a Dog," "Poem after Carlos Drummond de Andrade," "Sevens (Version 3): In the Closed Iris of Creation," and "Victim of Himself."

From *The Book of the Dead Man*: Preface, and poems #3, #14, and #23.

UNIVERSITY PRESS OF NEW ENGLAND publishes books under its own
imprint and is the publisher for Brandeis University Press, Brown University Press,
University of Connecticut, Dartmouth College, Middlebury College Press, Univer-
sity of New Hampshire, University of Rhode Island, Tufts University, University of
Vermont, and Wesleyan University Press.

Library of Congress Cataloging-in-Publication Data
Bell, Marvin.
    [Selections.    1994]
    A Marvin Bell reader : selected poetry and prose / Marvin Bell.
        p.        cm. — (The Bread Loaf series of contemporary writers)
    ISBN 0–87451–669–2. — ISBN 0–87451–670–6 (pbk.)
    I. Title.    II. Series.
PS3552.E52A6    1994
811'.54—dc20                                                  93–43937
⊗